Innovation Ecosystems
How Driving Forces and Success Factors
Affect Opportunities for Business Innovation

William B. Rouse

Routledge
Taylor & Francis Group

A PRODUCTIVITY PRESS BOOK

First published 2025
by Routledge
605 Third Avenue, New York, NY 10158

and by Routledge
4 Park Square, Milton Park, Abingdon, Oxon, OX14 4RN

Routledge is an imprint of the Taylor & Francis Group, an informa business

ISBN: 978-1-032-83041-4 (hbk)
ISBN: 978-1-032-83040-7 (pbk)
ISBN: 978-1-003-50746-8 (ebk)

DOI: 10.4324/9781003507468

Typeset in Garamond
by SPi Technologies India Pvt Ltd (Straive)

Contents

Preface

Over the past 50+ years, I have lived in a wide variety of places and have had 30 addresses. These 30 addresses can be clustered into eight geographical, social, and political ecosystems. In this book, I reflect on the similarities and differences among these eight ecosystems, including the trends that appear to be affecting them. These ecosystems are interdependent and progress has often depended on them advancing together rather than in competition.

Innovation Ecosystems is about people and places I have experienced, but it is not about me. Consequently, I do not report on why I was in these places or what I did while there. I highlight particular people, but only to provide context. I elaborate, often in some detail, the nature of the places discussed and typical activities that happen there, including how they compete and innovate.

This book is about geography, economics, society, and innovation. My favorite course in high school was economic geography. Why did different regions evolve in different ways? What caused economic priorities and activities to go in one direction or another? My sense is that happenstance played a relatively minor role in this process. There were and are driving forces, as well as success factors.

In each ecosystem, ambitious immigrants arrived, displaced native populations, and proceeded to develop and exploit the geography of their ecosystem, which included leveraging water resources for transportation, commerce, irrigation, etc. They often invented the means of development and exploitation, including unfortunately slavery, but also various technical methods, tools, and devices. Inventions that became innovations enabled industries, revenues, profits, and economic growth, initially for the ecosystem and then more broadly.

The impacts of geography and economics are profound. Available resources strongly affect the options available for sustainable economic growth. This growth is fueled by technological innovations that are significantly affected by the physical, economic, and social characteristics of the ecosystem of interest. The eight case studies in this book illustrate how patterns of these characteristics impact innovation.

The eight case studies depict changes over centuries, rather than just decades or years. Today's crises are often just blips in the ongoing evolution of an innovation ecosystem. There are ups and downs, but the physical, economic, and social characteristics of the ecosystems dominate their evolution. These factors largely determine what potential innovations are pursued, who leads these pursuits, and why they think they can succeed. People and organizations dominate the factors influencing success.

All of the descriptions of places are factual and based on a range of documentation, as well as experiences. Descriptions of people are factual as well, but portrayals of interactions among people are sometimes synthesized from minimal empirical evidence. My intent was to portray the spirit of the times to which these people richly contributed. Thus, there is a bit of creative non-fiction.

The stories in this book are inherently strongly influenced by my personal experiences. Indeed, the order of the chapters follows my lived experiences. These experiences are leavened with supporting evidence to the extent possible and reasonable. These personal experiences were profoundly affected by mentors and colleagues along the way. I am immensely grateful to the many people who befriended me, looked out for me, and provided guidance and advice. *Innovation Ecosystems* reflects the stories enabled by these relationships.

William B. Rouse
Asheville, NC

Author

**William B. Rouse** is Research Professor in the McCourt School of Public Policy at Georgetown University and Professor Emeritus and former Chair of the School of Industrial and Systems Engineering at Georgia Institute of Technology. His research focuses on mathematical and computational modeling for policy design and analysis in complex public–private ecosystems, with particular emphasis on healthcare, education, energy, transportation, and national security. He is a member of the US National Academy of Engineering and Fellow of IEEE, INCOSE, INFORMS, and HFES. His recent books include *From Human-Centered Design to Human-Centered Society* (Routledge, 2024), *Beyond Quick Fixes* (Oxford, 2023), *Bigger Pictures for Innovation* (Routledge, 2023), *Transforming Public-Private Ecosystems* (Oxford, 2022), *Failure Management* (Oxford, 2021), and *Computing Possible Futures* (Oxford, 2019). Rouse lives in Asheville, North Carolina.

Chapter 1

Innovation Ecosystems

Everyone thinks innovation is a good idea – will define it shortly. But, is the nature of innovation the same everywhere – for example, in technology versus the arts, or major urban areas versus smaller ecosystems? There are two answers to this question.

First, the nature of innovation depends on the context. Innovations in online gaming and classical music are far from identical. Second, the processes of invention and innovation are fairly similar, regardless of context. In this book, I elaborate and illustrate the nuances surrounding these two answers.

Innovation Ecosystems

Invention is the creation of a new device or process. Innovation is the creation of change in the marketplace. The marketplace can be for art, automobiles, computers, consumer products, or medicine, to name just a few ecosystems. The "market" may be a constituency rather than a commercial sense of marketplace.

From this broad perspective, innovation is context dependent. Some innovations are driven by inventions. Others are driven by needs – necessity is the mother of invention. New understanding drives others, for example, the discovery of bacteria. Similarly, mechanisms for the adoption of change vary by context.

DOI: 10.4324/9781003507468-1

Consider the differences between automobiles and medicine. The underlying phenomena are quite different. Automotive is driven by inventions in terms of characteristics of technologies, manufacturing processes, and value propositions. Medicine is driven by epidemics, war, and biomedical research. Both of these timelines are well understood.

Metrics depend on the context. Percentage of sales from new offerings makes sense for automobiles, but not healthcare delivery. The number of deaths avoided is likely a better metric for medicine. Increased Quality Adjusted Life Years is another metric. Notice the contrast. For automobiles, the key metrics are about what *did* happen – sales – while for medicine, the key metrics are about what *did not* happen – poor quality of life and deaths.

Given the contrasts I have drawn this far, what can we say about innovation in other arenas? Airplanes are much like automobiles. Education is much like healthcare. Let's add computing to the comparison. The following observations seem relevant:

■ Automotive: Devising means to make automobile driving easier, less expensive, more enjoyable, and safer – for consumers
■ Medicine: Discovering the causes of morbidity and mortality; and the understanding of how to thwart these causes – for patients
■ Computing: Developing means to solve complex computational problems for business and government – later for consumers

Innovations sometimes happen by crossing domain borders. Here are a few things that would not have happened without crossing borders.

■ Computing (1894) from Jacquard loom (1839)
■ Relativity (1915) and cubism (1907–1911) from geometry (1902)
■ Super Glue (1958) from glue that will not unstick (1942)
■ Electric lighting (1962) from light emitting diodes (1907)
■ Post-Its (1977) from glue that will not stick permanently (1968)
■ Internet (1991) from file sharing protocols (1983)

James Burke's *Connections* (Little Brown, 1978) elaborates on many more examples of border crossings. He reaches two general conclusions. First, the greatest impact of technology is hardly ever what the original inventor envisioned. Second, the greatest beneficiary of an innovation is rarely the original investor.

Differences among Domains

Innovations in consumer or business markets have long been my emphasis, but there can be innovations in, for example, scientific techniques. Of course, one could argue that the scientific community is then the market. Perhaps innovation happens when a targeted population changes how it does things.

In automobiles, we look at what people buy. In science, we look at what people cite. For consumers, we might look at what people consume or buy. In medicine, it may be clinicians voting, not patients. Same for expert service providers in general. Thus, the population of potential adopters targeted is key.

Another factor is the infrastructure needed to adopt something so it can become an innovation. This held up electricity but, once power plants and utility lines were in place, this eased the adoption of television – and many other inventions. A key to innovation, assuming needed infrastructure, is adoption by some population.

What does this mean in aerospace, automobiles, communications, computers, healthcare, medicine, etc., as well as art, education, economics, geography, history, humanities, politics, etc.? How do we measure innovation and visualize measurements in each of these domains? Let's start with just two domains.

Innovation in Technology

Does a technology trend change shape as the technology enables innovation, for example, corporate and venture investments in AI? The famous Gartner hype cycle model exhibits an interesting shape change in terms of expectations rather than adoptions. Clearly, there is not always a linear path from idea to R&D to innovation.

Chen Liu and I analyzed ten years of *IEEE Spectrum*'s annual issue on "Top Ten Tech Cars" to assess their abilities to predict innovations. We employed a huge data set of the exact configuration of each car sold globally over a decade. There were mixed results, probably meriting a grade of C. However, these annual special issues do raise expectations. This analysis also led to the realization that technology has "made it" when it is common on Honda Accords and Toyota Camrys, which have replaced Chevrolet Impalas and Ford Galaxies as the dominant platforms.

Gartner (www.gartner.com) defines the phases of the hype cycle as follows:

- A potential technology breakthrough kicks things off.
- Early publicity produces a number of success stories.
- Interest wanes as experiments and implementations fail to deliver.
- More instances of the benefits of the technology start to crystallize and become understood.
- Mainstream adoption starts to take off, as criteria for adoption are more clearly defined.

The hype cycle is an interesting representation of technological innovation. Expectations surge, propelled by exuberant marketing, plummet when expectations are not met, and eventually recover as value propositions mature and deliver real value. Eventually, innovations are absorbed into everyday life and we no longer think of them as innovations. Indoor plumbing and electricity are good examples.

The exuberance of marketing is relatively recent and is best illustrated by the current hype surrounding artificial intelligence (AI). In contrast, I could not find any *New York Times* articles portending the likely advent of indoor plumbing and electricity. It is interesting to imagine hype cycles for these important innovations. It took well over 50 years for Edison's vision to affect almost every home. It took over a century for the majority of homes in the developed world to have indoor plumbing. In contrast, the smart phone became ubiquitous in ten years.

How could the innovation of the smart phone happen so much more quickly? The answer, as noted earlier, is infrastructure. The smart phone could leverage the Internet and cellular technologies, not to mention electricity. Such infrastructure was not available to Edison, nor was it to Isaiah Rogers who first demonstrated indoor plumbing in 1829 in the Tremont Hotel in Boston.

The relevant metric here is quite straightforward. What percentage of the population is benefitting from the innovation? When every Accord or Camry comes with a backup camera as standard equipment, the camera technology has made it. When every vehicle has this capability, few could imagine a vehicle without it. Backup cameras, at this point, no longer seem like innovations.

Innovation in Art

Let's move from technology to art. Are there hype cycles for visual arts (painting, photography, sculpture), literature (fiction, non-fiction), performing arts (dance, improv, opera, symphony, theatre), and culinary arts? It is difficult to imagine anticipating the conceptual innovations of Picasso, Matisse, or Warhol, or the experimental innovations of Mondrian, Kandinsky, or Pollock. It is extremely unlikely that the usually prescient projections of *The Economist* would have heralded these innovations or that Gartner would publish hype cycles for art.

Innovation in art differs from innovation in technology. Only occasionally do these innovations involve technology adoption, for example, materials or techniques. Further, adoption does not mean that eventually everybody will embrace it. For instance, after Cubism emerged in 1907–1911, all the other artists did not become Cubists.

Orchestras that focused on Baroque music, for example, Bach, in the 17th century did not anticipate subsequent Classical music, for example, Mozart, and later yet Romantic music, for example, Chopin. There were no European fan magazines heralding the possibilities of these innovations. Yet, all three musical forms have endured as have indoor plumbing and air conditioning.

Innovation metrics for art might be adopted by art museums and orchestras. Once almost all orchestras included saxophones, invented by Adolphe Sax in 1841, one could argue this instrument was a genuine innovation. Similarly, once almost all major museums included exhibitions of Cubist art, you could say it had arrived.

I hasten to note that this is not how art historians view innovation. Instead, they would assess how the invention affected the artistic community. If other artists extolled the invention, despite not necessarily adopting it themselves, it would over time be seen as an innovation.

There are several significant differences between innovation in art and technology. Aesthetic innovation can involve creative adoption and extensions of old paradigms, sometimes abetted by technological innovations. Some artistic innovations involve leveraging technological innovations, for example, robots, for the purposes and intentions of these domains. However, technology is inherently different because of constant progress – few people want an innovative new outhouse.

A fascinating crossing of borders between technology and art involves the impact of Poincaré's famous book on geometry, which led to Einstein's relativity theory and Picasso's cubism. Science and art drew on the same intellectual roots to invent new conceptualizations of space and time. It would be quite difficult to imagine anyone having predicted these outcomes – unlikely that there would have been a hype cycle for geometry.

Measures of Innovation

Reviewing and contrasting innovations in technology and art, and considering how these observations apply to business, education, government, and law, the range of metrics has to broaden. For example, while innovations often involve adoption of technologies, they can involve new value propositions such as bundling or unbundling offerings, customer services, etc., and new approaches to marketing, sales, and service, as well as brick and mortar stores versus online.

For example, Nokia dominated the cell phone market providing less and less expensive phones globally. Apple came out with a $500 iPhone and took the market away. One could argue that Apple's innovation reflected the recognition that people wanted a general-purpose digital device that also included a phone; even though people did not yet fully know they needed this.

Technology innovations are the best documented with lots of plots of adoption curves. The rate of adoption is highly dependent on available infrastructure, for example, as noted earlier, power plants and utility lines for Edison and charging stations for battery electric vehicles. These adoption curves, such as with hype cycles, usually start from when the capability is first introduced to the market rather than when the enabling technologies were researched and invented, often many years earlier.

Typical measures of innovation include:

- Number of users or units sold/population of potential users – more people adopted smart phones than surgeons adopted robotic surgery
- Total revenues – very few aircraft carriers are sold, but they cost many billions of dollars
- Extent to which a technology, process, technique, etc. enables something that was previously impossible – a new medical device or new musical sound
- Extent to which humans' workflow, performance, safety, and health are significantly improved – reduction of medical errors and safety in crashes

■ Extent to which performance and appreciation of performance are substantially enhanced – speeds of race cars and quality of music

These contrasts emphasize the need to identify "markets" for inventions, ideas, new paradigms, etc. Whose acceptance and endorsement of an idea matters to an idea being deemed an innovation? Related issues are the size of markets and what other ideas are competing for adoption. Betamax would have become an innovation if VHS had not emerged from JVC and, in contrast to Sony, shared the technology with other firms.

Measures versus Domains

Table 1.1 presents three clusters of measures and maps them to six different innovation ecosystems. The three clusters are:

■ Performance – new, better, faster, cheaper
■ Market – market share, revenues, profits
■ Change – perceptions, attitudes, commitments, behaviors

Table 1.1   Relevance of Clusters of Measures to Different Domains

	Domains					
Metrics	*Arts*	*Autos*	*Educ.*	*Gov't*	*Med.*	*Tech.*
Does something new					√	√
Does it better					√	√
Does it faster					√	√
Does it cheaper					√	√
Impacts "market" significantly		√				√
Impacts market share		√				√
Impacts revenues		√				√
Impacts profits		√				√
Changes people's perceptions	√		√	√		
Changes people's attitudes	√		√	√		
Changes people's commitments	√		√	√		
Changes people's behaviors	√		√	√		

Innovations in medicine and technology relate to performance metrics. Innovations in autos and technology relate to market metrics. Innovations in art, education, and governments relate to change metrics. Within each cell of Table 1.1, especially for the change metrics, the perceptions, attitudes, commitments, and behaviors whose change would warrant designation as an innovation will depend on context.

Summary

The phenomenon of innovation seems broadly applicable, but the context matters in terms of the nature of what is considered innovative and how it is measured. New products, services, ideas, experiences, etc. have to be assessed and measured differently. Such considerations concern monitoring and projecting potential innovations.

Another essential concern is how best to foster innovation. In all domains, the vast majority of inventions do not lead to innovations. Most people and organizations are much more inventive than innovative, despite the claims on resumes and marketing brochures. Innovation is hard work.

Edison famously said, "Genius is one percent inspiration and ninety-nine percent perspiration." The perspiration is central to transforming a creative invention into a true innovation. The enthusiasms of many people and organizations wane when they come to realize this, whether they are artists, clinicians, or engineers.

Yet, there is another phenomenon that I have encountered working with hundreds of organizations. Many inventors simply do not believe that the inherently low probabilities of success apply to them. Consequently, they doggedly invest themselves, almost irrationally, in getting their creation to "market," whatever that means in their domain. While the odds remain very low, we all benefit from this determination and the few that actually become innovations.

Ecosystems Addressed

Over the past 50+ years, I have lived in a wide variety of places and have had 30 addresses. These 30 addresses can be clustered into eight geographical, social, and political ecosystems. The ordering of these eight ecosystems in Chapters 2–9 simply reflects the order in which I experienced them. My sense is that my interpretation of innovation in any particular ecosystem has inevitably been affected by the previous ecosystems encountered.

In this book, I reflect on the similarities and differences among these eight ecosystems, including the trends that appear to be affecting them. These ecosystems are interdependent and progress has often depended on them advancing together rather than in competition. Thus, they should not be viewed as independent samples in the sense one might argue were this a research study, rather than just a report from the field.

I have called each of these ecosystems home for at least one year, and for most of these ecosystems much longer. How are they similar and different? Tables 1.2 and 1.3 answer this question in terms of example innovations of each ecosystem driving forces and success factors affecting innovations.

Table 1.2 Example Innovations

Ecosystem	Example Innovations
Island	Ship design, underwater technologies & weapons
Shining City	Cybernetics, information theory, pragmatism
Heartland	Precision agriculture, vehicle & equipment manufacturing
Old Country	Global trade, water management
New South	AIDS treatment, supply chain management, retail
Gotham	Aviation, communications, computing, energy, fashion, finance
Capital	New Deal, Social Security, Medicare, Medicaid, vaccines
Mountains	Innovation Hubs, forest management, folk art

Table 1.3 Driving Forces and Success Factors

Ecosystem	Driving Forces	Success Factors
Island	Water & blue economy	Good work & delivering results
Shining City	Academic status & awards	Academic outcomes & recognition
Heartland	Agriculture & manufacturing	Good citizenship & outcomes
Old Country	Society & environment	Good citizenship & contributions
New South	Business results & consumption	Business formation & results
Gotham	Money, wealth & consumption	Connections, bluster & stories
Capital	Power & control	Relationships, credibility & deals
Mountains	Community, nature & art	Connecting & mentoring

The example innovations, driving forces, and success factors in these two tables will be explained in depth in Chapters 2–9. At this point, it is useful to highlight several contrasts. The examples in Table 1.2 are all rather different. The example innovations for each of the ecosystems have minimal overlaps, with the exception that they all involve people and money. Each ecosystem brings its own value propositions to their marketplaces. Thus, the stories elaborated in Chapters 2–9 are rather different, although there are some structural similarities as outlined at the end of this chapter.

Note that four of the ecosystems are large East Coast cities: Shining City (Boston), New South (Atlanta), Gotham (New York), and Capital (Washington). Over 1,000 miles separates these cities. To a great extent culture trumps geography in comparing the driving forces and success factors in Table 1.3 for these cities. Consider how these forces and factors differ.

All four cities are driven by pursuits of success. They all seek achievement, but this has different meaning in these four cities, at least as I have experienced these ecosystems. Boston defines itself in terms of academic achievement, perhaps not a surprise in a state with almost 150 colleges and universities. The higher education sector is the fourth largest in the state's economic base.

New York's achievement aspirations are totally focused on money. They are not concerned with producing anything tangible. The goal is money for money's sake. Their success is reflected in their conspicuous consumption. Elegant homes, expensive furnishings, designer clothes, and exquisite jewelry embody this great emphasis on consumption.

Atlanta is also completely focused on money as it accrues from profits creating tangible products, including software for marketing, sales, and operations. Consumption is also central, particularly in terms of enormous McMansions and high-end vehicles. Wheeling and dealing at boisterous college sporting events is a norm. Business networks are often aligned with alumni and religious affiliations.

Washington is concerned with achievement in terms of power and control. Relationships, personal credibility, and political deal making are central. Successful government service can pave paths to much better paying private sector jobs, perhaps later leading to higher-level government positions. Conflicts, infighting, and stalemates are common, but they seem to muddle through.

The other four ecosystems include The Island, Heartland, Old Country, and Mountains. These four contexts seem less focused on personal achievement than on society, community, and sustainability. Local concerns tend to be prioritized over personal wealth, perhaps because the opportunities for accruing enormous wealth are limited. We also need to keep in mind the inclinations of the people who choose to live or remain in each of the eight ecosystems.

Structure of Chapters

To facilitate comparisons across ecosystems, Chapters 2–9 are structurally similar. I begin by describing the early settlement of the region and, if relevant, colonization. I portray the primary cities and towns of the region, with an emphasis on being interesting rather than comprehensive. I summarize the economic base of each region.

Significant bodies of water – if relevant – are outlined. Means for crossing these bodies of water, by bridges, tunnels, and ferries, are summarized. The impacts of these bodies of water on the economics of each region are noted. Environmental threats related to these bodies of water are discussed. I show how the bodies of water across the eight ecosystems are related – and all end up in the Atlantic Ocean!

Several sections are tailored to the unique aspects of each ecosystem, including education, sports, arts, and culture. These sections tend to be difficult to compare across regions, with a couple of exceptions. For example, Gotham and Shining City emphasize professional sports, while Heartland and New South tend to be rabid about college sports.

The structure of the last three sections of each chapter is identical. The politics in each region are summarized, including how each addressed the Abolitionist Era (1790–1865), Progressive Era (1896–1917), and Civil Rights Era (1954–1968). As should be expected, each of the eight ecosystems addressed these eras quite differently. Challenges faced by each ecosystem are addressed in terms of economic, political, and environmental challenges.

A final section summarizes an innovation outlook for each ecosystem. Venture capital funding levels, relative to regional GDP, are described. Major growth opportunities are summarized, including an assessment of the region's prospects for successfully pursuing these opportunities.

These Innovation Assessments consider the prospects for each growth opportunity in terms of strengths, weaknesses, opportunities, and threats.

I outline in some detail context-specific strategies for pursuing opportunities and mitigating threats.

A final chapter, Chapter 10, contrasts the eight ecosystems in terms of an overall immigration story, sources of immigrants, and native populations displaced. I elaborate on the role of geography, particularly bodies of water. I trace the predominant bodies of water in the eight ecosystems to the Atlantic Ocean.

The markets served by each of the eight ecosystems are summarized. I then consider the overall ecosystem of the eight ecosystems in terms of producer–consumer relationships across the eight ecosystems, that is, the extent to which they serve each other.

These relationships are considered in more detail in terms of products, services, and people. Thus, the dependencies among ecosystems are more nuanced than a simple yes or no. They nurture each other in various ways.

I return to consideration of the driving forces and success factors introduced in Chapter 1. This provides a basis for exploring differences. The eight ecosystems illustrate the diversity of value propositions, ranging from underwater weapon systems on The Island to precision agriculture in Heartland to folk art and craft beers in The Mountains.

Such diversity is important across innovation ecosystems. If everyone tried to compete in the same way, everyone would be playing the same game. There would likely be a few big winners and many big losers. Fortunately, geography, natural resources, climate, and weather combine to discourage copycat innovators.

I conclude by integrating the Innovation Assessments across the 28 growth opportunities for the eight ecosystems. This integration is represented by four bar graphs of:

- Sources of competitive strengths
- Sources of competitiveness weaknesses
- Opportunities for competitive advantages
- Sources of competitive threats

The 112 assessments (i.e., 4×28) can be boiled down to a much smaller set of principles that govern innovation across seemingly disparate ecosystems.

Ecosystem Preview

For each of the eight ecosystems, there is a resource base of geography, knowledge, technology, and money that interacts with educational, government, and private sector enablers, all of which interact with nascent ecosystem innovations. Chapters 2–9 provide in-depth discussions of these relationships.

Figure 1.1 provides a summary view of ecosystem attributes as manifested in each of the eight ecosystems. I hasten to note that the brief bulleted lists below each ecosystem name are meant to be representative, not exhaustive. The chapter on each ecosystem provides much more information than can be incorporated into a single figure.

I return to this figure in Chapter 10 to explicitly contrast the ecosystems in terms of these attributes. The eight ecosystems have much in common, despite very different geographies, cultures, and politics. The nature of the innovations in each ecosystem varies significantly, but the processes of innovation have much in common across the ecosystems. Consequently, the ways in which driving forces and success factors affect opportunities for business innovation can be reasonably generalized.

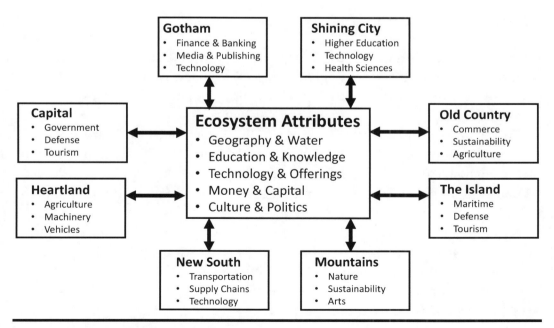

Figure 1.1   Ecosystem attributes.

Chapter 2

The Island

Aquidneck Island is the native American name for what colonial settlers named Rhode Island, The Island portion of the state of Rhode Island and Providence Plantations, the latter referring to the mainland. Voters chose to strip the words "and Providence Plantations" from Rhode Island's formal name in 2020 by approving a statewide referendum.

Before the Colonies

Narragansett Bay is a bay and estuary on the north side of Rhode Island Sound. The Bay forms New England's largest estuary, functioning as an expansive natural harbor, with a small archipelago extending into Massachusetts.

There are over 40 islands in the Bay. The three largest ones are Aquidneck, Conanicut, and Prudence Islands. Bodies of water that are part of Narragansett Bay include the Sakonnet River, Mount Hope Bay, and the southern, tidal part of the Taunton River. The Bay opens on Rhode Island Sound and the Atlantic Ocean.

Narragansett Bay is a "ria," a drowned river valley that remains open to the sea. It consists of a series of flooded river valleys formed in a horst and graben system that is slowly subsiding between a still-shifting fault system. This estuary system is vast compared to the present flow of the four small rivers that enter the Bay.

The present shape of Narragansett Bay is the result of the most recent glaciation of New England, under the edges of the Laurentide ice sheet at the Last Glacial Maximum, about 18,000 years ago. Sea level was lowered so

 DOI: 10.4324/9781003507468-2

much that the continental shelf was exposed, under its weight of ice, and the glacier calved into the Atlantic. Glaciers flowing through a geologically old sedimentary basin carved channels through the younger sediments and exposed much older bedrock.

Cuts gouged by the ice form the West Passage that separates Conanicut Island from the western mainland and the East Passage that separates Conanicut Island from Aquidneck Island. As the ice stalled, then retreated, the region became ice-free about 14,000 years ago. A complicated sequence of marine ingression and isostatic rebound flooded and emptied the land-scape. Salt water later filled the valley, as rising sea levels permanently flooded the area.

Following the retreat of North American glaciers, two tribes moved into the Bay area: the Narragansett to the west and the Wampanoag to the east. Both tribes still hold lands in southern New England and are federally recognized by the Bureau of Indian Affairs.

Wampanoag territory once extended from modern-day Boston in the north, to Warren, Rhode Island in the west, and eastward to the shores of Cape Cod, including Martha's Vineyard and Nantucket Island. The Wampanoag, which translates to "people of the dawn," had ample access to the shoreline and subsisted on fishing and agriculture.

The Narragansett, or "people of the small point," were known as warriors and frequently traded with other tribes across the region. Their territory once reached from the western shores of the Providence River and Narragansett Bay through regions of eastern Connecticut.

The first visit by Europeans to the Bay was probably in the early 16th century. It is accepted by most historians that the first contact by Europeans was made by Giovanni da Verrazzano, an Italian explorer who entered the Bay in 1524. He called the Bay "Refugio" (the "Refuge"). The Bay has several entrances, however, and the exact route of his voyage and the location where he laid anchor has led to uncertainty over which tribe made contact with him.

The Bay was explored and mapped by the Dutch navigator Adriaen Block in 1614, after whom nearby Block Island is named. The first recorded European settlement was in the 1630s, as described in the next section.

Roger Williams, a dissatisfied member of the Plymouth Colony, moved into the area around the year 1636. He made contact with the Narragansett sachem called Canonicus by the Europeans and set up a trading post on the site of Providence. In 1643, Williams traveled to England and was granted a charter for the new colony of Rhode Island.

Cities and Towns

Portsmouth was founded on the northern end of Aquidneck Island in 1638 by Anne Hutchinson with compatriots John Clarke and William Coddington, all of whom had been banished from the Massachusetts Bay Colony for not conforming to Puritan doctrines. They took boats across the Sakonnet River to land on Aquidneck Island. Rhode Island became a haven for such folks. The settlement was originally called Pocasset.

As noted above, two years earlier in 1636, Roger Williams, banished as well, had founded Providence Plantations on the mainland. One year later in 1639, Newport was founded on the southern end of Aquidneck Island. Over 100 years later, in 1743, Middletown was founded between Newport and Portsmouth, effectively dividing Newport's land area in two. I have often wondered if a more creative name could have been chosen. Of course, "new port" and "ports mouth" are not particularly creative choices either.

Anne Hutchinson, Roger Williams, and others came together to form the colony of Rhode Island and Providence Plantations. Rhode Island was the colonists' name for Aquidneck Island, the native Americans' name for The Island. The colony was one of the most liberal colonies, the home of the first Baptist church, the first Jewish synagogue, and one of the first Quaker meetinghouses.

As just noted, Newport was founded in 1639. Its eight founders and first officers were Nicholas Easton, William Coddington, John Clarke, John Coggeshall, William Brenton, Jeremy Clark, Thomas Hazard, and Henry Bull. Many of these people were part of the settlement at Portsmouth, along with Anne Hutchinson and her followers. They separated within a year of settling in Portsmouth and began the settlement of Newport on the southern side of The Island.

Newport grew to be the largest of the four original settlements that became the Colony of Rhode Island and Providence Plantations. The colony received its royal charter in 1663. Benedict Arnold was elected as the first governor. The Old Colony House at the head of Washington Square in Newport served as the seat of Rhode Island's government from 1741 until the current Rhode Island State House was completed in Providence in 1901. At that time, Providence became the state's sole capital city.

Newport became an important center of trade. Newport had 150 vessels engaged in trade and the manufacture of spermaceti candles, ships, barrels, rum, chocolate, textiles, clothes, shoes, hats, and bottles, as well as the slave trade. In 1727, James Franklin (brother of Benjamin Franklin) printed the Rhode-Island Almanack in Newport. In 1732, he published the first newspaper, the Rhode Island Gazette. In 1758, his son James founded the weekly newspaper Mercury. The famous 18th-century Goddard and Townsend furniture was also made in Newport.

Aquidneck Island was divided about in half between Newport and Portsmouth after Newport's founding in 1639. As noted earlier, Middletown was carved out of Newport's half of The Island and became a town on its own in 1743. Middletown was founded by the legislature in response to protests about inequities in the use of tax funds.

Jamestown was founded in 1678. Jamestown is situated almost entirely on Conanicut Island, the second largest island in Narragansett Bay. It also includes the uninhabited Dutch Island and Gould Island. The population was 5,559 at the 2020 census.

Prudence Island is the third largest island and is part of the town of Portsmouth. The Narragansett name for The Island was Chibachuweset. The Narragansetts sold The Island to Roger Williams and John Winthrop in 1637, with each man retaining a one-half interest. Williams took the northern side of The Island, and Winthrop took the southern side. Williams named it "Prudence" and shortly afterward purchased and named nearby Patience Island and Hope Island. As of the 2010 census, the population was 278.

The northmost portion of Portsmouth was developed as a summer colony. The Hummocks was founded in the 1890s, followed by Island Park just before the turn of the century, followed by Common Fence Point in 1925. Development of Island Park was accelerated by the creation of an amusement park or "trolley park" in 1898 when the Newport and Fall River Street Railway Company sought to increase ridership.

The park included a dance hall, beer hall, and dinner hall. The dance hall was right over the water and featured many nationally known bands. There was a carousel and shooting gallery. The *Bullet Ride* was the biggest rollercoaster in New England. The dinner hall filed for bankruptcy in 1927. The dance hall and beer hall were destroyed by fire in 1933.

On September 21, 1938, one of the most destructive and powerful hurricanes in recorded history struck Long Island and Southern New England. Designated the Great New England Hurricane of 1938, its 12-foot tidal waves surged up the Sakonnet River and destroyed the trolley park. All told, the hurricane killed 600 people and destroyed 6,000 homes. Eighteen people were killed in Island Park.

Economic Base

The Newport Naval Station is the predominant employer in Newport, with well over 10,000 employees and contractors. The US Navy has had a Newport presence since the Revolutionary War. The Naval War College was established in 1884. The Naval Academy was temporarily relocated in 1861–1865 from vulnerable Annapolis, Maryland, to Fort Adams during the Civil War. The Torpedo Station was established on Goat Island, in the Harbor of Newport, in the summer of 1869.

US NAVY AND NEWPORT

The relationship between Newport and the Navy goes back to before there even was a US Navy. Newport's naval history began with ships flying other flags. Giovanni da Verrazzano sailed into Narragansett Bay in 1524. The British Royal Navy occupied Newport from 1776 to 1779, despite an abortive attempt to evict them by the French in 1778. The French Navy would later decamp to Newport in 1780.

The outbreak of the Civil War in 1861 brought the US Navy's first permanent presence in Newport, when the US Naval Academy was temporarily relocated from vulnerable Annapolis. The Newport Naval Training Station opened in 1883 and the Naval War College in 1884.

The US Naval Torpedo Station was founded in 1869 and became the Navy's preeminent testing ground for torpedo technology. The Naval Undersea Warfare Center remains the Navy's top research, development, test, and evaluation center for submarine weapons systems.

The US Atlantic Fleet Cruiser-Destroyer Force was based in Newport from 1962 until the early 1970s, when it was relocated to Norfolk, Virginia. The departure of 40 ships and their crews plunged Newport into one of its darkest economic periods. The bars of Thames Street, once filled with sailors, emptied out, prompting Newport to reinvent itself as a tourist town.

The NUWC is the descendent of the Torpedo Station. NUWC is the United States Navy's full-spectrum research, development, test and evaluation, engineering, and fleet support center for submarines, autonomous underwater systems, and offensive and defensive weapons systems associated with undersea warfare. The Cruiser-Destroyer Force Atlantic was relocated from Newport to Naval Station Norfolk in the early 1970s.

Beyond the Navy, General Electric was a significant employer in Newport with 2,500 employees in RI. GE's withdrawal from RI was complete by 2000 because of high taxes and strong unions. There were no major employers in Portsmouth until Raytheon relocated its Submarine Signal Division in 1959 to be close to the US Navy in Newport, its major customer. This Raytheon Division once employed over 3,000 people but has scaled back significantly since the company's merger with United Technologies in 2020. I was an employee of this Raytheon Division during 1967–1969.

Weyerhaeuser (1926–1990) was never a large employer but The Island played an important role in the company's lumber supply chain. Its Portsmouth distribution facility was on the west shore of The Island on Narragansett Bay. Freight ships with rough cut lumber would dock at this finishing facility. The finished wood was delivered to lumber yards such as O'Connell's in Newport and Humphrey's in Tiverton.

Portsmouth once included large dairy operations at Glen Farm and Vaucluse Farm, both large "gentlemen's farms." There also has long been a very small agricultural economy for corn, potatoes, tomatoes, and a wide range of produce. Tourism is a major element of Newport's economy, accounting for over $1 billion in annual economic activity.

In 1809 the General Assembly announced a $10,000 lottery to develop a coal mine in the Narragansett Basin in Portsmouth. One million tons of coal were ultimately extracted from the mine. Heat and pressure made the anthracite coal in Rhode Island graphite rich and difficult to burn.

Portsmouth and Middletown have long been bedroom towns for Newport, Fall River, and Providence, as well as Boston. Portsmouth and Middletown are often acknowledged as great places to raise children, but young people tend to pursue their futures elsewhere.

Broader Context

Portsmouth was a small town in New England of 3,000 population in 1940, By 1950, the population had doubled to 6,000, reflecting growth driven by World War II. Yet The Island had long been rather isolated, accessible only by boat for nearly 300 years from its founding. Aside from the storm-challenged Stone Bridge, The Mt. Hope Bridge (1929), Sakonnet River Bridge (1956), and Newport Bridge (1969) integrated The Island into the state.

Currently, Newport County includes Newport (25,000), Portsmouth (17,000), Middletown (16,000), and to the east, across the Sakonnet River, Tiverton (8,000), and Little Compton (3,500). To the northwest, across

Narragansett Bay, are Bristol (22,000), Barrington (16,000), and Warren (11,000) in neighboring Bristol County.

Small Massachusetts cities include Fall River (94,000), New Bedford (101,000), and Worcester (206,000). All of these towns and cities operate within the Shining City ecosystem, a metro system of over 5 million people, and serve as bedroom residences for Boston and Providence.

Bodies of Water

The East Shore of The Island is defined by the Sakonnet River, a tidal strait between Mt. Hope Bay and RI Sound. The West Shore is defined by Narragansett Bay, a bay and estuary on the north side of RI Sound. These shores are referenced in this way, despite there being no official titles as such.

Mt. Hope Bay is a tidal estuary, an arm of Narragansett Bay, at the mouth of Taunton River, which flows through Massachusetts. Rhode Island Sound is a marine sound at the mouth of Narragansett Bay, a "sound" being a smaller body of water usually connected to a sea or an ocean, in this case the Atlantic Ocean.

Bridges over Bodies of Water

From the 1680s until 1795, when the Rhode Island Bridge Company built a wooden bridge in Island Park, a ferry shuttled goods, horses, wagons, and people across the Sakonnet River. The first bridge lasted two years before a high tide swept it away. The rebuilt bridge lasted one year, and ferry service resumed for a decade until subscribers raised $80,000. In 1810, travelers began to cross the new Stone Bridge constructed of 280,000 tons of stone at a cost of more than $200,000.

The Great Gale of September 1815 bit a 200-foot chunk out of the bridge, and a gale in 1868 caused a similar breach, prompting the state to take control of a new, toll-free bridge in 1871. The free bridge became a popular spot for hooking striped bass, bluefish, and shark, with one reported landing of a 500-pounder.

Trolley cars from the Newport and Fall River Street Railways began crossing the bridge in 1898, which required replacing the old wooden draw with iron and steel strong enough to hold 20 tons.

On the Tiverton side of the bridge, a village of stores, fish markets, and blacksmith shops blossomed. For more than 100 years, a succession of inns at the foot of the bridge served weary travelers and hosted milestone celebrations for town residents until the 1980s, when the Stone Bridge Inn was razed.

The last car crossed the Stone Bridge on May 6, 1957. The Hurricane of 1938 and Hurricane Carol in 1954 weakened the bridge's approaches and caused service interruptions, leading to the construction of the steel Sakonnet River Bridge about a half-mile north of the Stone Bridge. The first Sakonnet River Bridge was opened in 1956. In ill repair due to lack of maintenance, it was replaced in 2012 by a bridge with the same name.

It was not the first or last bridge. The Mt. Hope Bridge opened in 1929, replacing the Bristol Ferry, which had commenced in 1680 off Bristol Ferry Road. This ferry was the quickest way to Providence, which became the RI State Capitol in 1901. Route 114 stretches from Aquidneck Island through Bristol, Warren, and Barrington to Providence.

The Newport Bay Bridge opened in 1969, replacing the Jamestown Ferry from Newport to Jamestown. Travel to South County, for example, the University of RI in Kingston, required taking Jamestown Ferry until 1969, or going the long way through Providence, or even longer through Fall River to Providence and then south. As a student at the University, I received a year-round pass on the ferry for one dollar.

Many Island natives still bemoan the fact that the bridges were ever built as they facilitate tourist traffic, unwanted by some, but not everybody. This grouchy cohort tends to include folks who refer to going "off island" whenever they travel to the mainland.

Trolley Line

Aquidneck Island was once served by two electric-powered street railways or trolleys. From their beginning in 1898 and continuing until 1925, the three island communities were serviced by two major lines. The routes served were somewhat obvious, following the East Main Road and the West Main Road. At its peak of service, one line extended from Newport's Fifth Ward to Bristol Ferry via the West Main Road and the other out the East Main Road from One-Mile Corner to the Stone Bridge and Tiverton.

In 1898, construction of a "Trolley Park" began in Island Park. As noted earlier, this was an amusement park, built by the trolley company to encourage ridership from both north and south. This park thrived in the first third of the 20th century as a major Saturday or Sunday afternoon adventure for people from as far away as Fall River or Newport. However, after several fires and especially the 1938 hurricane, the park was destroyed.

Trolleys were well used. The Newport and Providence passenger count peaked in 1919 with 2.7 million riders. Between 1902 and 1911, the Old Colony Line served from 2.8 to 3.2 million riders each year. But the decline set in very quickly in the 1920s. Trolley service was gradually replaced by buses and, of course, the persistence of the automobile was a fatal blow to mass transit as well. The number of trolley runs shrank as other methods of travel grew. The last Newport to Fall River run took place on February 28, 1925, and on May 26, 1925, all regular trolley service ceased in Newport.

Fall River Line

Beyond the Navy presence noted above, Newport was also a center of commercial maritime industry. The Fall River Line operated between New York City and Boston from 1847 to 1937, with its base of operations in Newport. J.P. Morgan and the New York & New Haven leased the Old Colony Railroad in 1892 and gained effective control of the Fall River Line. By 1898, there were no longer any independent lines, and consolidation of in the steamboat market was mostly complete. J.P. Morgan had a relationship with the line until a 1914 federal settlement forced the railroads to divest of coastal steamboat lines.

The trip from Boston to Fall River, Massachusetts, was by train; from Fall River to New York was by steamboat through Narragansett Bay and Long Island Sound. Its steamboats were among the most advanced and luxurious of the time and a highly popular means of travel. Newport was a major stop in both directions.

George Peirce was a legendary builder of passenger ships for routes between Boston and New York City. His best-known ships were the Puritan, Pilgrim, Providence, and Priscilla, which was called the Queen of Long Island Sound. His ships were elegant, luxurious, and on the leading edge of technology. His son, Charles, led the electrification of the ships, eliminating the kerosene lamps that often led to ship fires.

Charles Peirce subsequently joined Edison Electric, which soon became General Electric (GE) formed by J.P. Morgan orchestrating the merger of Edison Electric and Thomson-Houston Electric Company in 1892. Peirce became an executive in the railway division of GE and led the electrification of the first railway in the United States, the Nantasket Line.

America's Cup

Another maritime venture has been the America's Cup, which began in 1851 and is considered the oldest trophy for any international sport. In August of 1851, America raced against 15 yachts of the Royal Yacht Squadron in the club's annual regatta around the Isle of Wight. America won, finishing 8 minutes ahead of the closest rival. John Cox Stevens and his brother Edwin A. Stevens built and skippered the winning yacht, *America*.

From 1930 to 1983, the races were sailed off Newport for the rest of the reign of the New York Yacht Club (NYYC). In 1958, after a halt in America's Cup sailing due to World War II, the 12-meter yachts brought a new era of America's Cup racing to Newport from 1958–1983 until, for the first time in 130 years, the NYYC lost the Cup to Australia. From June 23 to July 1, 2012, the America's Cup World Series was held inside Newport Harbor after a 20-year absence.

Newport is home to the National Sailing Hall of Fame and America's Cup Hall of Fame, located in the space once used as the Press Room for the America's Cup. It was founded in 2022. The International Tennis Hall of Fame also resides in Newport, opening in 1954. It is located in the Newport Casino, which was commissioned in 1879 and designed by Charles McKim along with Stanford White.

Newport Summer Cottages

The Gilded Age was a period of rapid industrialization in America from 1865 to 1898. It was characterized by the extreme concentration of wealth in a few individuals. Many others lived in poverty. Political corruption and exploitation of immigrant labor are often associated with this era.

Newport played a major role during this period, between roughly 1870 and 1910, as some of the world's wealthiest people came to the "City-by-the-Sea" to build summertime "cottages" along the waterfront. The Breakers, perhaps the most famous cottage, included 70 rooms. Cornelius Vanderbilt II, grandson of the innovator, built this cottage. I revisit this cottage in the last few paragraphs of this book.

Many of the cottage owners lived in New York City. The society section of the *New York Times* had a Newport section each week indicating which of the cottage owners would be in Newport for the coming weekend. For example, the February 22, 1896 and July 3, 1896 issues of the *Times* reported that "Mr. Frederic P. Vinton, the well-known artist of Boston, and Mrs. Vinton were visiting Mr. and Mrs. George Peirce in Newport." Vinton's wife Annie was the daughter of George and Mary Peirce.

People could travel from Boston or New York to Newport on the elegant Fall River Line which, as noted above, was led by George Peirce and owned by a J.P. Morgan company. It is easy to imagine the Vintons traveling to and from Newport in this manner.

Ocean Drive, also known as Ten Mile Drive, encompasses most of the southern coastline of Aquidneck Island. Many of the "cottages" were built on this dramatic stretch of road facing the Atlantic Ocean. Ocean Drive intersects with Bellevue Avenue, which hosts many other substantial "cottages."

Newport Jazz Festival

The Newport Jazz Festival is an annual American multi-day jazz music festival held every summer in Newport. Elaine Lorillard established the festival in 1954, and she and her husband Louis Lorillard financed it for many years. They hired George Wein to organize the first festival and bring jazz to Rhode Island.

In 1972, the Newport Jazz Festival was moved to New York City. In 1981, it became a two-site festival when it was returned to Newport while continuing in New York. The festival was hosted in Newport at Freebody Park, but crowding led to its relocation to Fort Adams State Park. Louis Armstrong, Mahalia Jackson, Duke Ellington, and John Coltrane were among the many headliners in the 1960s that I was fortunate to hear play.

Newport Folk Festival

The Newport Folk Festival is an annual American folk-oriented music festival in Newport, which began in 1959 as a counterpart to the Newport Jazz Festival. The festival was founded by music promoter and Jazz Festival founder George Wein, music manager Albert Grossman, and folk singers

Pete Seeger, Theodore Bikel, and Oscar Brand. It was one of the first modern music festivals in America and remains a focal point in the expanding genre of folk music.

The festival was held in Newport annually from 1959 to 1969, except in 1961 and 1962, first at Freebody Park and then at Festival Field. In 1985, Wein revived the festival in Newport, where it has been held at Fort Adams State Park ever since. Stars of the 1960s that I was fortunate to hear included Joan Baez, Bob Dylan, and Peter, Paul and Mary.

Portuguese Immigrants

Rhode Island was a preferred destination for Portuguese immigrants. They were not new to the state. Before the Civil War, a number of Azoreans and Cape Verdeans who had arrived on whaling ships stayed on after the whaling industry declined, to work in the Providence and New Bedford textile mills, or became farmers in Portsmouth or Little Compton.

Between 1897 and 1921, almost 20,000 Portuguese immigrants (more than half of them actually from the Azores) named Rhode Island as their intended residence. After World War II, there was another wave of Portuguese immigration to the country; many were fleeing the right-wing dictatorship of Antonio Salazar. These immigrants became mill workers in Fall River or farmhands in Portsmouth.

Their work ethic prevailed, and many were soon small business owners. Their children often became politically active. By the third generation, many offspring were becoming doctors, lawyers, and engineers. They steadily moved up the economic ladder and were increasingly successful. Yet their roots remained strong as evidenced by the enduring St. Anthony's Feast.

The St. Anthony's Feast at the Portsmouth Portuguese American Citizens Club is a long-standing tradition, virtually as old as the club itself. The club was founded in 1927 for the betterment of the Portuguese people and culture in Portsmouth.

> The feast is not as culturally Portuguese as it was in decades past, but there are chorizo sandwiches. There are also the rides, games and music, the trappings one would expect to see at any festival, not just a Portuguese one. Thirty years ago it was more of a traditional Portuguese event.

Island Politics

Since the Great Depression, Rhode Island politics have been dominated by the Rhode Island Democratic Party and the state is considered part of the Democrats' "Blue Wall." Democrats have won all but four presidential elections since 1928, with the exceptions being 1952, 1956, 1972, and 1984.

Rhode Island is ranked as one of the most unionized states in the country. According to a new report on full-time workers from the Bureau of Labor Statistics (BLS), nonunion workers earned just 82% of the median weekly amount that union member workers earned. Rhode Island is not a right-to-work state. Therefore, union membership can be a condition to employment.

Recent legislative victories in Rhode Island include a full suite of domestic violence laws and a prohibition on ghost guns and high-capacity magazines. The Ocean State ranks number 13 nationally in gun law strength and experiences the fifth-lowest gun death rate. Rhode Island prohibits any person from carrying a handgun (concealed or visible) on or about the person without a license, except in their dwelling house or place of business or on land the person possesses. Carrying a handgun without a license is prima facie evidence of an intention to commit a crime of violence and is admissible evidence in a prosecution for a crime of violence.

Rhode Island has an affirmative right to abortion enshrined in state law. Upon the Governor's signing of the act in May of 2023, the Lt. Governor Sabina Matos observed, "This victory for equity in health care was only possible due to the passionate advocacy of the citizens who made their voice heard year after year here at the State House."

Abolitionist Era

Newport anti-abolitionist leaders had an active material interest in an economic system rooted in slavery, and they fought to uphold that system. The anti-abolition sentiment was also rooted in an anti-blackness that had long permeated colonial New England. Nevertheless, Rhode Island was a key player in the abolitionist era.

Rhode Island began to phase out slavery with gradual abolition in 1784, but did not eradicate it until 1842. The abolitionist sentiment was strong and growing. An artist and spiritualist tried to recruit a budding naval hero, Matthew Perry.

Gilbert Stuart (1755–1828) was North Kingston born and a celebrated portrait painter, most notably of George Washington. William Ellery

Channing (1780–1842) was a Newport born leader of the Unitarian move-ment. In a chance meeting at the White Horse Tavern, America's oldest restaurant, serving guests since 1673, they encountered a fairly young Newport born Matthew Perry (1794–1858).

This discussion in the 1820s, fairly early in Perry's career, seemed to influence his subsequent impacts. Matthew Perry later commanded the African Squadron to suppress slave trading in 1843–1844. He then com-manded the squadron that opened trade with Japan in 1852–1854. Never an ardent abolitionist, he nevertheless had an impact on the movement. He is buried in Island Cemetery in Newport with many other city luminaries.

Progressive Era

The focus of the Progressive Era was on reforming the excesses of the Gilded Age. Perhaps the most visible progressive was Theodore Roosevelt (1858–1919) who was elected Vice President under William McKinley, serving until September 1901. He became President upon McKinley's assas-sination and served for 1901–1909.

Roosevelt had been Assistant Secretary of the Navy during 1897–1898 and was a major advocate of the Navy. In late 1904, he was in Newport for a meeting at the Naval War Cottage. Sarah Elizabeth Doyle (1830–1922), Providence-born advocate for women's education at Brown and founder of the RI School of Design, was conducting a progressive workshop the next day at Channing Memorial Unitarian Church, founded in 1835 and renamed for Channing in 1881.

Doyle had recruited Ida Tarbell (1857–1944), a leading muckraker and reformer of the Progressive Era, as her keynote speaker on her book *History of the Standard Oil Company* (1904), then being serialized in *McClure's*. She had also tried, without success, to recruit Jane Addams (1860–1935), founder and leader of social settlement services by Hull-House in Chicago.

One of the congregation members at Channing Memorial knew Roosevelt rather well and reported that he was in Newport, visiting the Naval Station. She had suggested to Doyle that they invite Teddy to make a brief appearance and offer some supportive words. He surprisingly agreed and obviously had done his homework, praising the efforts of Tarbell and Doyle, as well as Addams who he had not realized would not be there. The whole event was a complete success.

Civil Rights Era

The Summer White Houses in Newport in the late 1950s and early 1960s played a role in the middle of civil rights debates. President Dwight Eisenhower, an avid golfer, had located his summer residence during 1958–1960 on a corner of Fort Adams to be close to the Newport Country Club, which opened in 1893.

Senator John Kennedy often visited Hammersmith Farm, his wife's childhood home, which would become his Summer White House during 1961–1963 when he was elected President. When in Newport, Kennedy often played golf at the Newport Country Club. It was inevitable that Eisenhower and Kennedy would encounter each other.

One encounter, which was difficult to confirm, involved a discussion about the emerging civil rights movement. Eisenhower counseled Kennedy that Martin Luther King (1929–1968) was going to be a major player in civil rights, in fact leading the movement during 1955–1968. Kennedy was very supportive of civil rights, but his assassination led to President Lyndon Johnson leading the charge to the Civil Rights Act of 1965.

Challenges

All ecosystems face challenges – economic, political, and environmental. The Island has some idiosyncratic elements of these challenges due to its having been a Gilded Age playground, its strong Navy presence, and the omnipresence of several bodies of water.

Economic Challenges

The financial panics of 1873 and 1893 caused the Gilded Age to wane in Newport and more broadly. These financial panics also motivated Progressive Era changes. The Great Depression (1929–1939) demolished the lingering remnants of the Gilded Age. Newport, as the playground of the Gilded Age, experienced significant economic decline.

Rhode Island experienced a more severe downturn during the Great Recession (2007–2009) than any other New England state. Rhode Island also saw steeper house price declines during the recession than any other New England state. Rhode Island had larger job losses across its economy than any other New England state and may have contributed to the larger shock to its financial sector.

Political Challenges

These challenges have primarily involved wars. The British occupied The Island during the Revolutionary War (1776–1779). The Battle of Rhode Island was fought on August 29, 1778. The battle took place in Portsmouth and was the only major action of the war that took place in Rhode Island. The battle was tactically inconclusive in its outcome. The British failed to overwhelm the American force, which continued its orderly retreat from The Island.

The Revolutionary War decimated The Island's economy due to a lack of trade. The British destroyed much of the city's housing and caused a large depression in its economy. They left in 1779, taking a number of prominent Tory merchants with them. The French arrived in Newport in 1780, bringing hard currency with them, whereupon some of the colonial merchants returned.

The island had limited involvement in the War of 1812. Island industry contributed to supplies during the Civil War. Newport hosted the Naval Academy during the war as it was relocated from Annapolis.

During World War I, Newport was a major contributor to training. A German U-boat surfaced in Newport Harbor in 1916, before the United States had entered the conflict. During World War II, Newport was again a major contributor to training, but was also a major player in torpedo production.

During the Korean War, Newport remained a major contributor to training. For the Vietnam Conflict, Newport trained South Vietnamese naval officer candidates. Newport remains a major Navy training center.

Environmental Challenges

Climate change and global warming pose a wealth of challenges. Hurricanes have been The Island's greatest environmental challenges. Hurricanes, of course, become more intense as ocean temperatures rise.

> ***1938 Great Hurricane***. The storm surge was especially violent along the Rhode Island shore, sweeping hundreds of summer cottages out to sea. Narragansett Bay's funnel shape drove the storm surge to almost 16 ft. In Jamestown, seven children were killed when their school bus was blown into Mackerel Cove.

Many homes and structures were destroyed along the coast, as well as many structures inland along the hurricane's path, and entire beach communities were obliterated on the coast. The boardwalk along Easton's Beach in Newport was completely destroyed by the storm.

A few miles from Conanicut Island, Whale Rock Light was swept off its base and into the waves. The Prudence Island Light suffered a direct blow from the storm surge, which measured over 17 feet. The light keeper's home was utterly destroyed and washed out to sea. The light keeper's wife and son were both killed.

The original parchment of the 1764 Charter of Brown University was washed clean of its text when its vault was flooded. There was clear evidence that this was the strongest hurricane to hit Rhode Island in over 300 years. The Fox Point Hurricane Barrier was completed in 1966 because of the massive flooding from the 1938 storm and from the even higher surge that resulted from 1954's Hurricane Carol.

> *1954 Hurricane Carol*. On August 31, 1954, Hurricane Carol came ashore on the coast of Newport, RI with a massive surge and winds of 115 mph. In one hour, Carol destroyed 3,800 homes, sank or damaged 2,000 boats and yachts, and leveled almost all of the island's power and telephone lines.

While the storm was less powerful than the 1938 hurricane, Carol was still able to destroy many of Newport's coastal attractions, such as the Merry-Go-Round at Easton's Beach and Johnny's Atlantic Beach Club. All of Rhode Island lost electrical power due to the storm, and 65 people were killed in Southern New England. The hurricane left in its wake over $200 million in property damage in Rhode Island alone.

Innovation Outlook

Where is Aquidneck Island headed? To put this question in context, first consider where Rhode Island is headed. How much is being invested in growth opportunities and which opportunities seem most promising?

Venture Capital Funding

Consider the venture capital dollars invested in each state, relative to the state's nominal gross domestic product (GDP). According to *US News*, the ranking of the New England states is MA (1, tied with CA), VT (5), CT (17),

RI (31), NH (33) and ME (41). Of course, Rhode Island's GDP of $71 billion, compared to Connecticut's $253 billion and especially Massachusetts' $688 billion, suggests a different scale of their economies. On the other hand, Vermont's $41 billion shows that a small state can compete.

Growth Opportunities

A study conducted by Battelle, Brookings, and Deloitte in *Sizing the Clean Economy: A National and Regional Green Jobs Assessment* (2011) suggested the top growth opportunities for each state. Rhode Island's top three opportunities included the following:

Life Sciences. "Rhode Island is strong in biomedical innovation, advancing scientific knowledge of biological processes and systems in ways that are reshaping the diagnosis and treatment of medical conditions. There are particularly attractive market opportunities in neuroscience-related therapeutics; medical devices for orthopedic, bio-sensing, and neurological applications; and healthcare informatics and digital innovations.

Biomedical innovations are converging with technology development in other scientific fields – including electronics, information technology, imaging, and nanoscience – to offer new insights that inform the creation of biomedical products. Biomedical innovation requires close collaboration between basic research, clinical research, and industry development, all of which is easily facilitated in Rhode Island."

IT Software, Cyber-Physical Systems, and Data Analytics. "The convergence of technologies such as wireless communications, sensing, imaging data and cyber-physical systems is generating strong and ever-evolving consumer demand. Rhode Island companies are advantageously perched on the cutting edge, thanks to the state's strengths in engineering, design, data analytics, cybersecurity, and computer science. Rhode Island's collaborative environment means technological innovations are applied across industries. Specific growth opportunities include cyber-physical systems and data analytics, autonomous underwater vehicles, remote medical device monitoring systems, environmental and energy monitoring, and smart grid infrastructure."

Blue Economy. "This is an area where Rhode Island has long dominated. The state is home to a wide range of maritime industries, including boat building and servicing; home to the largest independent steamship agency in North America; defense-related ship and submarine building; development of advanced materials and component boat/ship systems; ocean sciences and engineering; marine tourism; and the preservation of coastal communities and environments. A highly integrated maritime economy that encompasses manufacturing and research reinforces the competitive advantages of the Ocean State."

How does all of the above relate to Aquidneck Island? Consider what is needed to compete in the above three growth opportunities. Strong STEM (science, technology, engineering, and mathematics) competencies are required. Brown University and the University of Rhode Island, with enrollments of 11,000 and 18,000, respectively, are the two major players in this arena, neither of which is situated on Aquidneck Island. Brown has the only medical school in the state.

This suggests the Blue Economy is the sweet spot for Aquidneck Island, which makes sense given the dominance of the surrounding bodies of water and the long-standing major presence of the US Navy. One can easily argue that major investments, including those by the State, should focus on the strong growth of the Blue Economy. This is already a priority at the University of Rhode Island, but Massachusetts, in particular, has similar aspirations.

I mentioned that the "best and brightest" among K-12 and college graduates often felt compelled to leave the state, often lured by the Shining City addressed in Chapter 3. This is not necessarily a negative phenomenon. After all, Rhode Island is often characterized as a suburb of Boston. Nevertheless, Rhode Island in general and Aquidneck Island in particular could benefit from increased entrepreneurial zeal.

Innovation Assessment

Table 2.1 summarizes the strengths, weaknesses, opportunities, and threats for each growth opportunity of the innovation outlook for The Island. There are significant risks that warrant some deep strategic thinking and planning.

This ecosystem is in a strong position for Blue Economy, especially if it can expand beyond defense, leveraging URI's outstanding ocean engineering program. This would mitigate the risk of depending on one large customer, who can relocate (Navy) or merge (Raytheon).

Life Sciences can build on some strengths such as Brown and URI, but is in the shadow of the juggernaut in Boston and Cambridge. A good strategy would be to partner with the Massachusetts innovators, perhaps by

Table 2.1 Innovation Assessment for the Island

	Innovation Outlook		
	Blue Economy	*Life Sciences*	*Software & Systems*
Strengths	Incumbency Newport Navy	Universities in RI Innovators in MA	Track Record with Defense
Weaknesses	Labor Unions & High Taxes	Nascent Market Position	Labor Unions & High Taxes
Opportunities	Expand Beyond Defense	Partner with MA Innovators	Expand Beyond Defense
Threats	Dependency on One Major Client	Very Crowded Marketplace	Very Crowded Marketplace

identifying niches where high value offerings would be attractive to these larger innovators.

Software & Systems can build on a strong track record with defense customers, but needs to broaden beyond defense. Perhaps the other two growth areas can be leveraged to integrate deep subject matter expertise with technical skills.

The main challenges for all these growth areas are high taxes and labor costs, which provide opportunities for low-cost competitors to preempt market penetration. Such competitors are likely to be outside New England and perhaps offshore.

Epilogue

Growing up on an island on the seacoast of New England seems like a storybook beginning. Indeed, it was. It took me a long time to realize how sheltered I was by oceans, beaches, fields, and forests. I did not realize at the time how lucky I was to be able to freely roam and discover my little world.

I was anxious to move to the Shining City, to broaden my explorations. I imagine that I thought I would then understand the broader world. However, as the other chapters in this book chronicle, there was eventually much more discovery on the agenda. In fact, I would come to explore over 50 countries.

I limited consideration in this book to ecosystems where I actually lived as I think that day-to-day life can be informative in different ways than mere visits. One can learn the rhythms of a place. Nevertheless, one's understanding of any particular place is inevitably affected by the other places one has deeply experienced.

Thus, there is a path dependence on the accumulation of insights. Living in Boston and then later New York City, rather than in the opposite order, at the very least affects whether you root for the Celtics and Red Sox or Knicks and Yankees. It also affects your preferences for pasta, pizza, and beer.

Chapter 3

Shining City

Puritan John Winthrop's lecture, "A Model of Christian Charity," was delivered in 1630 in Southampton before his first group of Massachusetts Bay colonists embarked on the ship Arbella to settle Boston. Winthrop warned his fellow Puritans that their new community would be "as a city upon a hill, the eyes of all people are upon us."

John Kennedy echoed this theme in his inaugural speech in 1961 and Ronald Reagan in his speech in 1980 and subsequently in 1989, adding shining city and referring to Washington, DC. In this chapter, I apply this appellation to Boston as originally intended.

Pre-colonial Society

Various English, French, and Italian explorers visited the Northeast between the 15th and 17th centuries, either looking for a suitable location for a colony or looking for a passageway to the east. The Native Americans living in New England at the time had mixed reactions. Some tribes welcomed them with open arms while other tribes were less friendly, which made exploration treacherous. These expeditions laid the groundwork for future English and French colonization in North America during the 17th century.

There are two federally recognized tribes within Massachusetts: the Wampanoag Tribe of Gay Head and the Mashpee Wampanoag Tribe. These Massachusetts tribes are the descendants of the original people that the English invaders first encountered. The Mashpee Wampanoag Tribe,

DOI: 10.4324/9781003507468-3

also known as the People of the First Light, has inhabited present-day Massachusetts and Eastern Rhode Island for more than 12,000 years.

Relations between the colonists and Native Americans worsened over the course of the 17th century, resulting in a bloody conflict known as the First Indian War, or King Philip's War. In 1675, the government of the Plymouth Colony in Massachusetts executed three members of the Wampanoag people.

The execution of these three Wampanoag men, for murdering an Indian informant, precipitated the war, but war had been likely as the English settlements pushed farther west. Thousands of Native Americans were killed, wounded, or captured and sold into slavery. Decades after the Wampanoag helped the English survive in their lands, they were now enslaved by those very people. Slavery is addressed in more detail later in this and other chapters.

An arduous process, lasting more than three decades, resulted in the Mashpee Wampanoag being re-acknowledged as a federally recognized tribe in 2007. In 2015, the federal government declared 150 acres of land in Mashpee and 170 acres of land in Taunton as the Tribe's initial reservation, on which the Tribe can exercise its full tribal sovereignty rights. The Mashpee tribe currently has approximately 2,600 enrolled citizens.

Formation of Colony

Plymouth Colony (1620–1691) was the first permanent English colony in New England. It was settled by the passengers on the Mayflower at a location that had previously been surveyed and named by Captain John Smith.

The Massachusetts Bay Colony (1628–1691) was an English settlement on the east coast of North America around Massachusetts Bay, one of the several colonies later reorganized as the Province of Massachusetts Bay.

The Province of Massachusetts Bay was a colony in New England that became one of the 13 original states of the United States. It was chartered on October 7, 1691, by the joint monarchs of the kingdoms of England, Scotland, and Ireland and was based on the merging of several earlier British colonies in New England.

The charter merged the Plymouth Colony, the Massachusetts Bay Colony, the Province of Maine, Martha's Vineyard, Nantucket, Nova Scotia, and New Brunswick. The Commonwealth of Massachusetts is the direct successor. Maine became a separate state in 1820. Nova Scotia and New Brunswick were parts of the colony until 1697 when they became Canadian provinces.

Cities and Towns

Boston was founded in 1630. It is well-known for its many colleges and universities – 64 in metro Boston. Prominent institutions within the city proper include Boston College, Boston University, Northeastern University, Simmons College, and the University of Massachusetts.

The Museum of Fine Arts on Huntington Avenue is world renown. Well-known Boston painters include landscape painter Winslow Homer (1836–1910) and portrait painters John Singer Sargent (1856–1926) and Edward Porter Vinton (1846–1911). Sargent's portrait of Vinton is exhibited in the Rhode Island School of Design Museum.

Symphony Hall on Massachusetts Avenue is home to the Boston Symphony Orchestra and the Boston Pops. The legendary Arthur Fiedler (1894–1979) conducted the Pops, followed by the equally legendary John Williams (1932). Boston Pops concerts on the Esplanade on the Charles River have long been very popular.

The Boston Common is a public park in downtown Boston. Founded in 1830, it is the oldest city park in the United States. It includes 50 acres of land. The Boston Public Garden is a large park adjacent to the Common across Charles Street. Founded in 1837, it features rich and unusual plants, the Lagoon, monuments and fountains, and the Swan Boats that have operated for over 100 years.

From the Common one can follow the Freedom Trail to Faneuil Hall. For nearly three centuries, Faneuil Hall has been a prominent meeting location for residents and visitors to Boston and a central point of commerce for the city. In 1742, the nation's forefathers proclaimed it "The Cradle of Liberty."

Further along the Freedom Trail is the open-air Haymarket Farmers' Market. Operated by the Haymarket Pushcart Association, its history traces to 1820. Roughly 50 Haymarket vendors sell fruits, vegetables, and seafood at very low prices, obtained from wholesale distribution terminals north of Boston. Prices are low because the wholesale markets need to make room for frequent new shipments.

The Rose Fitzgerald Kennedy Greenway is the park over the O'Neill Tunnel discussed below. It enables walking from the area of the Farmers' Market to the North End, Boston's Little Italy, a maze of narrow streets with some of the city's oldest buildings. Also on the Freedom Trail, it passes historic sites like the 1680 Paul Revere House and the Old North Church, which played a key role at the beginning of the Revolutionary War. Italian restaurants, coffee-houses, and pastry shops pack the area, particularly on Hanover Street.

Cambridge, also founded in 1630, is across the Charles River from Boston. It is home to Harvard University, founded in 1636, as well as the Massachusetts Institute of Technology (MIT), founded in Boston in 1861 and moved to Cambridge in 1916. Well-known neighborhoods include Harvard Square and Brattle Street near Harvard and Kendall Square near MIT.

Medford was founded in 1630 as part of Charlestown, but became independent in 1892. It is home to Tufts University, which includes the Fletcher School of Law and Diplomacy, a graduate school of international affairs and one of America's oldest graduate schools of international relations. I was a faculty member at Tufts following my graduation from MIT.

North of Boston are the seacoast towns of Marblehead (1645), Salem (1626), and Gloucester (1642). South of the city are Cape Cod and the islands of Martha's Vineyard (1641) and Nantucket (1641). Provincetown, at the tip of Cape Cod, was founded in 1727.

Prominent military bases in metro Boston include Hanscom Air Force Base in Bedford and the Natick Army Soldier System Center. Joint Base Cape Cod houses all five military services, on the site of the original Otis Air Force Base and Army Camp Edwards. I served my active duty in the Air Force as a 2nd Lieutenant at Hanscom Air Force Base.

Economic Base

Massachusetts' GDP is $700 billion, ten times that of Rhode Island. The state has a highly diversified economy, hosting headquarters of 17 of the Fortune 500 companies. By way of comparison, California, New York, and Texas each host roughly 50 of Fortune 500 corporate headquarters.

The largest industries by revenue include pharmaceuticals, for example, typified by Kendall Square, cosmetics and toiletries, for example, Gillette, life insurance and annuities, for example, State Street Bank, and colleges and universities, with 150 private and public institutions in the state.

Representative current companies include General Electric ($76B revenue), which was founded in Schenectady, NY in 1892 with J.P. Morgan involved; headquarters moved to Boston from Fairfield, CT in 2016. Raytheon Technologies ($71B) was founded in Boston in 1922 by Vannevar Bush and others; headquarters moved to Washington, DC in 2022. Smaller representative companies include Boston Scientific ($13B), which has been in greater Boston since 1979, and Gillette ($10B), which was founded in Boston in 1901.

GILLETTE

The Gillette company and brand originated in the late 19th century when salesman King Gillette came up with the idea of a safety razor that used disposable blades. The idea was to, effectively, give away razors, but sell blades. While Gillette came up with the idea in 1895, developing the concept into a working model and drawings that could be submitted to the Patent Office took six years. Gillette had trouble finding anyone capable of developing a method to manufacture blades from thin sheet steel, but found William Emery Nickerson. Gillette and other members of the project founded the American Safety Razor Company in September 1901. Production began slowly in 1903, but the following year Nickerson succeeded in building a new blade grinding machine to relieve bottle-necked production. During its first year of operation, the company sold 51 razors and 168 blades, but the second year saw sales rise to 90,884 razors and 123,648 blades. The company was renamed the Gillette Safety Razor Company in 1904. In 2005, Procter & Gamble announced the largest acquisition in its history to buy Gillette in a $57 billion deal. The deal combined some of the world's top brands. P&G was the largest consumer products company in the world.

Route 128 semi-circles Boston and has been known for technology innovation since World War II. Raytheon has many operations in the vicinity of Route 128. Digital Equipment Corporation (DEC) was founded in Maynard in 1957 and grew to be ranked 38th in the Fortune 500 in 1988 with roughly $10B in sales. The founder and CEO, Ken Olsen, dismissed the personal computer market. DEC was acquired by Compaq and Intel in 1998.

Data General was a spin-off from DEC in 1968, headquartered in Westborough along Route 128. They were one of the first minicomputer firms of the late 1960s. They reached over $1B in revenue but also missed the personal computer market. Data General was acquired by EMC in 1999. DEC and Data General illustrate how innovators often succumb to Schumpeter's "creative destruction."

Broader Context

The academic ecosystem of Boston includes many top universities, as noted earlier. Harvard and MIT in Cambridge epitomize this ecosystem. Harvard grads have become 24 heads of state, 31 heads of government, 78 US cabinet secretaries, 95 US state governors, 120 US senators, and 393 US representatives. This is clearly an impressive and influential lineup.

MIT's central role in science and technology has resulted in many Nobel prizes and comparable accolades. The Institute's role in business formation has been exemplary. A 2015 report underscored the substantial economic impact of MIT's faculty and alumni entrepreneurs, whose companies – over 30,000 as of 2015 – have created millions of jobs and generated annual revenues of nearly $2 trillion.

MIT has been a major player in business formation, but is far from the only player. My later relationships as a faculty member and advisory board member with MIT, Stanford, University of California (UC) at Berkeley, UC Los Angeles, UC San Diego, University of Illinois (Chapter 4), Delft University of Technology (Chapter 5), and Georgia Tech (Chapter 6) have repeatedly evidenced the potential of science and technology to have pervasive economic impacts, particularly when institutions are both excellent and have the scale to execute.

Thus, the Shining City serves as an outstanding exemplar of how academic ecosystems can motivate and enable innovation, both via faculty and alumni excellence, and also due to a steady stream of highly qualified and ambitious graduates.

Bodies of Water

Boston Harbor is a natural harbor and estuary of Massachusetts Bay, consisting of 50 square miles with 180 miles of shoreline and 34 harbor islands. The Inner Harbor includes the mouths of the Charles and Mystic Rivers, Chelsea Creek, and the port of Boston; the Outer Harbor includes the three bays of Dorchester, Quincy, and Hingham and the mouth of the Neponset River.

The entire harbor is relatively shallow, on average less than 20 ft deep. To maintain its commercial viability, it is routinely dredged in key areas to maintain suitable depth for large craft. The main channel that runs through President Roads between Deer Island and Gallops Island, then into the Inner Harbor and Mystic River Basin industrial port, is maintained by dredging to support container ships. The Boston Harbor Deep Draft Navigation Project dredges the channel to 47 ft depth.

The Massachusetts Bay extends for over 40 miles from Cape Ann in the north to Plymouth Harbor in the south on the eastern coast of the Commonwealth. It is a major feature of the North Atlantic Ocean and is part of the greater Gulf of Maine ecosystem.

Crossing Bodies of Water

There are over 100 bridges that cross the 80 miles of the Charles River. Tobin Bridge is one of several that cross the 7 miles of Mystic River from Medford to Boston Harbor. It is the longest bridge in Massachusetts. The Neponset Bridge is one of several that cross the 29 miles of Neponset River from Foxborough to Dorchester Bay.

Significant tunnels include the Ted Williams Tunnel under Boston Harbor, providing access to Logan Airport. The O'Neill Tunnel is not under water, but runs under downtown Boston. It is the result of the "Big Dig," more formally the Central Artery/Tunnel Project. Costing $24 billion over 16 years, the project was plagued by cost overruns, delays, leaks, design flaws, charges of poor execution and use of substandard materials, criminal charges and arrests, and the death of one motorist.

Ferries of note include the Boston-Provincetown Ferry and the Woods Hole Ferry to Martha's Vineyard and the Nantucket Ferry between Hyannis and the island. The time from Boston to Provincetown is 90 minutes. The trip to Martha's Vineyard is 45 minutes, while the trip to Nantucket requires 135 minutes. The two island ferries serve almost 4 million passengers per year.

Higher Education

For the academic year 2022–2023, 146 colleges and universities are active in Massachusetts – 42 public and 104 private schools. I highlight two in this section, Harvard University and MIT.

Harvard, founded in 1636, cultivated a wealth of intellectual innovations over almost four centuries. One is particularly interesting. Transcendentalism is an American literary, philosophical, religious, and political movement of the early 19th century. Transcendentalists were critics of their contemporary society for its unthinking conformity and urged that each person find an original relation to the universe.

By the 1840s they, along with other transcendentalists, were engaged in a range of social experimentation and, by the 1850s, in an increasingly urgent critique of American slavery. Transcendentalism is closely related to Unitarianism, a religious movement in Boston in the early 19th century. It started to develop after Unitarianism took hold at Harvard University. My family has long been Unitarian.

Transcendentalism became a coherent movement and a sacred organization with the founding of the Transcendental Club in Cambridge, Massachusetts, in September 1836. Prominent members included Ralph Waldo Emerson, Bronson Alcott, Margaret Fuller, and Henry David Thoreau. Emerson and Thoreau sought their relationship with the universe in solitude amidst nature, and in their writing.

Late in this period, a most fascinating relationship emerged between William James (1842–1910), a Harvard faculty member in the Department of Psychology, and Charles Sanders Peirce (1839–1914), a Harvard graduate who lectured at Harvard and was, for several years, a faculty member in the Department of Mathematics at Johns Hopkins University.

The James-Peirce dialog has been captured in their frequent correspondence and interactions. Their discourse centered on pragmatism. Peirce claimed that truth is "the opinion which is fated to be ultimately agreed to by all who investigate" while James claimed that truth "is only the expedient in the way of our thinking." It is widely agreed that James and Peirce are among America's most original thinkers.

Harvard Business School (HBS) was founded in 1908. It consistently ranks among the top business schools in the United States and globally. Particularly relevant to the main theme of this book is the work of HBS faculty member Clayton Christensen. His book *The Innovator's Dilemma* (HBS Press, 1997), as well as subsequent books, chronicle the difficulties of displacing incumbent, albeit inferior, product and service offerings.

MIT was founded in Boston in 1861 and moved to Cambridge in 1916. The last few decades of the 19th century were a rich time for founding institutes of technology, including Massachusetts (1861), Stevens (1870), Georgia (1885), and California (1891). MIT's move to Cambridge solidified that city's claim to academic fame.

The history of MIT is laced with luminaries, the Institute's faculty and alumni having won roughly 10% of all Nobel Prizes. Vannevar Bush (1890–1974) was a technology visionary, whose vision led to the formation of the National Science Foundation. He also was a co-founder of Raytheon.

Norbert Wiener (1894–1964) pioneered the field of cybernetics, the science of communication and control theory that is concerned with automatic control of both technical and biological systems. Claude Shannon (1916–2001) provided fundamental contributions to information theory, the mathematical study of the quantification and communication of information. Weiner and Shannon were contemporaries and it is easy to imagine their dialogs addressing the interactions of their theories.

Paul Samuelson (1915–2009) was the first American to win the Nobel Prize in Economic Sciences in 1970. MIT faculty or alumni have now won 12 Nobel Prizes in Economic Sciences, just one behind Harvard's 13 and ahead of Chicago's 9. Cambridge is obviously a great place for Nobel Prizes in Economic Sciences.

MIT has a long tradition of visionary Presidents. Karl Compton and James Killian both played important roles in Washington during World War II and the Cold War. As an MIT alum, I have met several MIT Presidents. However, my in-depth experiences were with Charles Vest (1941–2013), President of MIT (1990–2004) and President of the National Academy of Engineering (2007–2013). He stands as one of my heroes.

Sports

Bostonians are avid sports fans, much more of professional sports than college sports. Their teams have rewarded their support. The Celtics have won 17 NBA Championships. The Red Sox have won 9 World Series. The Patriots have won 6 Super Bowls. The Bruins have won 6 Stanley Cups.

Perhaps the best-known players of each team are Bill Russell (1934–2022) of the Celtics, Ted Williams (1918–2002) of the Red Sox, Tom Brady (1977) of the Patriots, and Bobby Orr (1948) of the Bruins. Acknowledged by many as perhaps the best hitter in baseball history, Williams played in only one World Series (1946), which the Red Sox lost to the St. Louis Cardinals.

Russell and Williams were contemporaries and would occasionally interact. There is a story that Williams asked Russell if he agreed that the hardest task in sports is hitting a 100-mph fastball. Russell responded that this task is certainly very difficult, but even more difficult is winning 11 championships in 13 years. If Tom Brady had been there, he might have argued that winning 7 Super Bowls was very difficult as well.

City Politics

Four US presidents were born in Massachusetts:

- John Adams – 2nd US President (1797–1801). Born in Braintree in 1735
- John Quincy Adams – 6th US President (1825–1829). Born in Braintree in 1767
- John F. Kennedy – 35th US President (1961–1963). Born in Brookline in 1917
- George H. W. Bush – 41st US President (1989–1993). Born in Milton in 1924
- George Bush was a surprise to me. I would have guessed Connecticut where his father was a US Senator.

As noted earlier, John Winthrop was the first governor of the Massachusetts Bay Colony. There have been two Massachusetts Representatives who served as Speaker of the House. Joseph W. Martin (1884–1968) was the only Republican Speaker of the House between 1931 and 1995 – elected twice in 1947–1949 and 1953–1955. Thomas (Tip) P. O'Neill (1912–1994) was Democrat Speaker of the House (1977–1987).

Well-known US Senators who did not become President included Henry Cabot Lodge, Sr. (1893–1924), Henry Cabot Lodge, Jr. (1947–1953), Edward Brooke (1967–1979), and Edward Kennedy (1962–2009). Of course, Massachusetts has had many distinguished US Senators.

Elliot Richardson, a Republican, spent an interesting decade in government as Lt. Governor of Massachusetts (1964–1966), Attorney General of Massachusetts (1966–1969), US Secretary of Health, Education and Welfare (1970–1973), US Secretary of Defense (1973), and US Attorney General (1973), ending with Richard Nixon firing him for refusing to fire special prosecutor Archibald Cox, who was charged with prosecuting the Watergate break-in.

Liberal Republicans Extinct

Richardson, the Lodges, and Brooke were liberal Republicans – liberal socially and conservative fiscally. John Chafee in RI and Nelson Rockefeller in NY were two others. Such Republicans no longer exist.

Richard Nixon's "southern strategy" to win the presidency in 1968 involved courting white supremacists, particularly in southern states.

He focused on their fear and anger regarding cultural elites, immigration, and assimilation. He won and, over time, the mass of southern Democrats became southern Republicans.

Nixon was forced to resign in 1974 due to Watergate. However, his messaging on white supremacy has persisted. Donald Trump built on this legacy almost 50 years later to win the presidency in 2016. Richardson, the Lodges, Brooke, Chafee, and Rockefeller would not recognize today's Republican Party.

Central Issues

For each ecosystem, I consider how they addressed the Abolitionist Era, the Progressive Era, and the Civil Rights Era. Not surprisingly, the Northeast and South held very different positions.

Abolitionist Era. The Massachusetts Historical Society's *Boston Abolitionists 1831–1865* (https://www.masshist.org/features/boston-abolitionists/) provides a summary. "Boston became a center of the national antislavery movement, and in 1831 William Lloyd Garrison, committed to the cause, began publication of *The Liberator*, the country's leading abolitionist newspaper. The New England Anti-slavery Society supported immediate abolition and viewed slavery as immoral and non-Christian. It was particularly opposed to the American Colonization Society, which proposed sending African Americans to Africa."

Progressive Era. James Connolly in *The Triumph of Ethnic Progressivism: Urban Political Culture in Boston, 1900–1925* (Harvard, 1998) indicates that "Bostonians came together to define a vision for their city's future and created 'Boston – 1915 Plan,' a reform drive spearheaded by retail magnate Edward A. Filene and muckraker Lincoln Steffens. Launched in 1909, the 1915 Plan sought to present an image of Boston after six years of progressive reform, as a goal for all citizens of the city to pursue. Steffens argued that if people were to be lured away from allegiance to corrupt bosses, they needed another magnet for their loyalties. Activist women throughout the country, from Boston in the East, to Seattle in the West, and Memphis in the South, focused on improving public schools, especially in poor neighborhoods."

Civil Rights Era. *The Encyclopedia of Boston* (https://boston researchcenter.org/projects/encyclopedia-of-boston/) provides a summary. "Though racial segregation was not codified by law in Boston, it was an unofficial policy in the city, one reinforced by the Boston School Committee's decisions. Schools in African-American neighborhoods were badly underfunded, underequipped, and understaffed, eliciting protests from enrolled students and their parents. Schools that served black children received about two thirds of the amount of funding received by schools in white neighborhoods.

In 1963, 8,000 people marched through Roxbury to protest "de facto segregation" in Boston's public schools. In April 1965, Martin Luther King Jr. led a march from Roxbury to Boston Common to protest school segregation. In response to decades of racial segregation, in 1974, the U.S. District Court for the District of Massachusetts required the Boston Public Schools to integrate the city's schools through busing.

Court-mandated busing, which continued until 1988, provoked enormous outrage among many white Bostonians, and helped to catalyze racist violence and class tensions across the city throughout the 1970s and 1980s. Anti-busing protests and iconography became national news in these years, and cemented Boston's reputation as a city plagued by racial and socioeconomic strife."

Challenges

All ecosystems have economic, political, and environmental challenges, but the nature of these challenges tends to differ based on the characteristics of the ecosystem. *Confronting Boston's Challenges* (https://cssh. northeastern.edu/bari/challenges-facing-boston/) summarizes the challenges being faced by the Shining City.

Economic Challenges

"Boston is currently experiencing two overlapping housing crises. The first is an immediate crisis due to the pandemic and ensuing recession. The second derives from a long period of tremendous economic growth across the region that outpaced regional housing production. The reasons for the high costs of housing are many: inflation, land costs, labor, and materials. Even Boston's prosperity and affluence work against renters. According to Boston's Office of Housing, an individual making $78,550 a year is considered 'low-income' when applying for income-restricted housing opportunities."

Political Challenges

"Social challenges include issues such as food insecurity, housing instability, financial strain and employment instability in their families. The majority (52%) of Massachusetts residents and their families had at least one unmet health-related social need in 2019. More than 2,000 Massachusetts voters were recently surveyed, and 43% singled out jobs and the economy as the most pressing issue facing the country. When the same survey was conducted in 2020, the coronavirus was the top issue for 51% of respondents."

Environmental Challenges

"In addition to water pollution due to industrial, commercial, and residential wastes, Boston faces an air pollution problem due to the city's transportation and commercial sectors. These sectors pump various different types of greenhouse gases, chemicals, and other harmful pollutants into the air based on the needs of the system that they are using. In the coming decades, the Boston area is likely to see more intense storms, more hot days, and rising sea levels."

Innovation Outlook

World War II had a profound effect on Boston. Research revenues dramatically increased at Harvard and MIT. Defense companies prospered. New starts, such as Digital Equipment Corporation (DEC), emerged in 1957. During the same period, the textile industry moved south causing deindustrialization and resulting in unemployment. Lower costs of labor, facilitated by a lack of unions in the south, as well as increased levels of automation, motivated companies to move.

The "Massachusetts Miracle" was a period of economic growth in Massachusetts during most of the 1980s when Boston recovered. The unemployment rate fell from more than 12% in 1975 to less than 3%, which was accompanied by tax reductions and a drastic increase in personal income. Beyond DEC, notable companies founded included Apollo Computer, Data General, Lotus Development Corporation, Prime Computer, and Wang Laboratories.

The growth was heavily centered in financial services and high-tech industry – often enabled by technology from Harvard University and

MIT – both within Boston and in its suburbs along Route 128. The name of the road has been used as a nickname for the regional tech economy, much like Silicon Valley, which grew rapidly beginning in the 1950s with strong encouragement from Stanford University.

Another notable region in the Raleigh-Durham-Chapel Hill area of North Carolina is called the Research Triangle because of its proximity to three major research universities – Duke, the University of North Carolina at Chapel Hill, and North Carolina State University – as well as being a hub for technology and biotech companies. The Research Triangle also began in the 1950s with strong encouragement from the three universities.

More recently, the economy of Boston has felt and is recovering from the effects of the pandemic. Commuting into downtown Boston has fallen dramatically as people work from home. This has hurt restaurant, retail, and hospitality business. Strong job growth has occurred in sectors where remote work is more feasible. Fortunately, as outlined below, Boston is well positioned for sustained economic growth.

Venture Capital Funding

Silicon Valley receives roughly a third of all venture capital funding – $23 billion in 2016. New York is second with 11%. San Jose and Boston each receive 10%. Los Angeles gets 8%. So, two-thirds of all venture capital funding goes to just five ecosystems. For life sciences, San Francisco is first, Boston second, and San Diego a distant third. Everyone experienced a decrease in venture capital funding in 2022, plausibly due to changing business practices during the pandemic. Nevertheless, Boston is well positioned for funding, especially in life sciences.

Growth Opportunities

The companies formed during the Massachusetts Miracle in the 1980s were primarily computer hardware and software companies. Many of these companies, including DEC and Data General, were acquired in the 1990s and 2000s as this industry consolidated, leaving Apple and Microsoft dominant today. Primary growth opportunities are in newer areas rather than these traditional markets.

Greater Boston (https://massecon.com/our-regions/greater-boston/) reports that "Boston economic development is flourishing, effectively making this area an economic leader across New England and the world.

Undeniably regarded as one of the world's greatest life sciences cluster and a leading financial center, Boston continues to be a hub of global innovation and growth. One of the greatest assets of the region is its highly educated workforce. The workforce in this area attracts the best and brightest talent, including 350,000 college students who annually come from around the world to matriculate in Boston and Cambridge."

"The city's professional and financial services sectors, such as information, professional, scientific, and technical services, and finance and insurance, showed resilience to the economic recession with modest but positive real growth in 2020. In 2021, these sectors continued their growth trend and contributed more than half of the city's 7 percent real increase from 2020 to 2021."

"Payroll employment in professional, scientific and technical services in 2022 stood 9.1% above its pre-pandemic level, with manufacturing (6.4%), information (5.4%) and health care and social assistance (2.6%) also seeing job increases over 2020. Job gains have been led by scientific research and development (up 36 percent since 2020), management and technical consulting services, software publishing, and computer systems design and related services."

Strategy consulting services has long been a strong suit. Boston Consulting Group ($11 billion annual revenue) and Bain ($6 billion) are headquartered in Boston. They compete with McKinsey ($15 billion), headquartered in New York. Accenture, Deloitte, EY, KPMG, and PwC also operate in Boston, but do not primarily compete with these strategy specialists. These larger firms often use strategy engagements to gain access to much larger opportunities to, for example, lead IT implementations.

"Hiring in professional and technical services, information, and health care and social assistance has continued to push past pre-pandemic levels. Many of these jobs are connected to Boston's life science research cluster which continues to be a key driver both for labor demand and real estate investment."

"Boston continues to be one of the top NIH funded cities in the nation, ranking second behind New York City in the 2022 fiscal year. Boston received 4,329 awards to its various independent hospitals, research institutes, and universities for a total of $2.4 billion in funding. Five of the top ten funded hospitals in the U.S. are located in Boston – Massachusetts General Hospital, Brigham and Women's Hospital, Boston Children's Hospital, Dana-Farber Cancer Institute, and Beth Israel Deaconess Medical Center. MGH was the highest funded hospital in Boston, as well as the nation, with almost $560 million in grants. MGH grants make up approximately 24 percent of Boston's NIH funding."

"The Boston Planning & Development Agency approved 4.7 million square feet of new lab space in 2022, and construction permits were issued for projects totaling 5.4 million square feet of non-residential construction. Though the Boston office market has softened, with vacancy increasing to 10.8 percent in the fourth quarter of 2022, lab space has remained a bright spot for commercial development in Boston."

An important advantage of the Shining City innovation ecosystem is its demonstrated ability to move into new arenas, for example, life sciences vs. computers, as older areas mature, while also sustaining investments in legacy segments where competitive advantages can be retained, for example, consulting, financial services, and higher education. This enables embracing creative destruction rather than pretending that it is not happening.

Innovation Assessment

Table 3.1 summarizes the strengths, weaknesses, opportunities, and threats for each growth opportunity of the innovation outlook for Shining City. Clearly, this ecosystem is in a very strong position in terms of incumbency, reputation, and very long track records of success. Of course, these opportunities are very attractive to other players. The main overarching challenge is high taxes and labor costs, which provides opportunities for lower-cost competitors to edge into these markets.

Table 3.1   Innovation Assessment for Shining City

	Innovation Outlook			
	Life Sciences	*Financial Services*	*Professional Services*	*Higher Education*
Strengths	Incumbency Installed Base	Incumbency Reputation	Incumbency Reputation	Incumbency Installed Base
Weaknesses	High Taxes & Labor Costs	High Taxes & Labor Costs	High Taxes & Labor Costs	High Taxes & Labor Costs
Opportunities	Expand Market Offerings	Sell Expertise Globally	Sell Expertise Globally	Premier Online Offerings
Threats	Global Competition	Global Consultants	Global Consultants	Global Competition

Epilogue

My move to the Shining City in 1969 transformed my life. First, it immediately reconnected me with my family roots in Boston. I had only traveled to Boston a couple of times before my move, despite it only being one hour away. Nevertheless, I had thoroughly digested stories of family exploits in Boston.

One story involved my great-grandfather, Charles Peirce, attending MIT in 1882 and being attracted away by the high-tech industry in 1884, eagerly seeking electrical engineering expertise. It took the family 87 years to return! My mother, in particular, was thrilled.

The intellectual culture at MIT was and is compelling. I had done very well as an undergraduate in engineering at URI. However, so did all the other graduate students. Consequently, the competition was intense.

Fortunately, the overall levels of confidence among these students were so high they were quite willing to help each other. This led to many friendships that have persisted for over 50 years. These friendships were celebrated at coffee shops and pubs, but also were leveraged for business opportunities sometimes characterized as "deals."

Immersion in innovation ecosystems, as I have experienced in the eight instances in this book, results in amazingly rich networks of relationships that can provide ideas, insights, critiques, and often opportunities. You can gain enormously from these relationships, and these networks gain power by leveraging you. It can be – and has been – amazingly symbiotic.

Chapter 4

Heartland

The first humans in Illinois arrived around 8000 BC. Over time, these people developed agriculture alongside hunting and gathering. Around AD 1000, North America's most complex civilization north of Mexico developed along the Mississippi, centered in the city of Cahokia, directly across the Mississippi River from present-day St. Louis, Missouri, near the confluence of the Missouri, Illinois, and Mississippi rivers.

Cahokia was the center of a trading network linked to other societies over much of North America. It was the largest and most influential urban settlement of the Mississippian culture, which developed advanced societies across much of what is now the Central and Southeastern United States, beginning more than 1,000 years before European contact. The Cahokia Mounds State Historic Site is the site of a pre-Columbian Native American city that existed roughly 1050–1350.

Before Settlers

When European explorers first entered the land now called the State of Illinois, they encountered a people who became known to the world as the Illinois or Illiniwek Indians. The Illinois were a populous and powerful nation that occupied a large section of the Mississippi River valley. They became important allies of French fur traders and colonists who came to live among them, and they played a key role in the early history of what would later become the midwestern United States.

The world of the Illinois was turned upside down during their long association with French settlers and later British and American colonists.

 DOI: 10.4324/9781003507468-4

As time passed, their population declined and many of their traditional ways of life changed as they adapted to new situations. Eventually, the Illinois were forced to leave their traditional lands and move west to Indian Territory. Their descendants, the Peoria Tribe of Indians of Oklahoma, are now scattered throughout the United States but maintain their tribal headquarters in Miami, Oklahoma.

The first Europeans to visit Illinois were the French explorers Louis Jolliet and Jacques Marquette in 1673, when they explored the Mississippi and Illinois rivers. Near present-day Peoria, René-Robert Cavelier, Sieur de La Salle, established the first French foothold, Fort Crèvecoeur, and built Fort Saint Louis near Ottawa. In the 1760s, after the French and Indian War, France ceded to Britain its claim to lands east of the Mississippi.

British policy was unfavorable to the area's economic development. Native Americans resented the British presence, and settlements were without civil government. By 1773 the number of settlers had declined to about 1,000 plus a few hundred slaves. In 1778, during the American Revolution, the capture by American forces of Kaskaskia, the British seat of government in the region, made Illinois a county of Virginia.

The first settlement on the site of Chicago was made in 1779 by the black pioneer Jean-Baptist-Point Du Sable. On July 4, 1800, the Northwest Territory was divided, and the Illinois country was made a part of Indiana Territory. Illinois Territory was formed in 1809 by dividing Indiana Territory, and Illinois attained statehood in 1818.

Cities and Towns

The population of metropolitan Chicago is 9.5 million, while the city proper is 2.7 million. The population of the state is 12.7 million. Thus, three-quarters of the people live in or near Chicago. The largest Illinois cities outside of metropolitan Chicago have populations of roughly 100,000 or so. Thus, small cities and their rural surrounds dominate the state's geography. The nature of this primarily non-urban innovation ecosystem is my emphasis in this chapter.

Chicago

Nevertheless, Chicago deserves some mention. The third largest city in the United States was founded in 1837, abutting Lake Michigan. Chicago is renowned for its architecture, particularly skyscrapers. Notable cultural venues include the Chicago Symphony Orchestra, once directed by the legendary Sir Georg Solti, the Lyric Opera of Chicago, the Art Institute of Chicago, and the Field Museum of Natural History.

Water Tower Place is a large urban, mixed-use development comprising a 758,000 sq ft shopping mall in a 74-story skyscraper in Chicago. The mall is located on North Michigan Avenue, along the Magnificent Mile, Chicago's premier commercial district. This area is home to upscale shops, fashion outlets, cool restaurants, and posh hotels. Landmarks include the historic Chicago Water Tower, the neo-Gothic Tribune Tower, the terracotta Wrigley Building skyscraper, and the John Hancock Center.

Two particularly notable universities are Northwestern University in Evanston and the University of Chicago in Hyde Park. Founded in 1851, Northwestern focuses on art and science, social science, engineering, journalism, law, management, medicine, music, medicine, and performing arts studies. Founded in 1890, University of Chicago scholars have played a major role in the development of many academic disciplines, including economics, law, literary criticism, mathematics, physics, religion, sociology, and political science. Both universities are very highly ranked.

Springfield

Founded in 1821, Springfield is the state capital. I traveled there often when conducting research for the Illinois State Library. The State Library provides support to over 3,370 public, academic, school, and special libraries throughout Illinois that together comprise the Illinois Library and Information Network (ILLINET).

The Lincoln Home National Historic Site preserves the home and related historic district where Abraham Lincoln lived from 1844 to 1861, before becoming the 16th president of the United States. Also in Springfield are the Abraham Lincoln Presidential Library and Museum and Lincoln's Tomb.

Quad Cities

The Quad Cities is a region of four cities in the states of Iowa and Illinois: Davenport (1836) and Bettendorf (1903) in southeastern Iowa and Rock Island (1841) and Moline (1848) in northwestern Illinois. Before Europeans arrived, the confluence of rivers had attracted many varying cultures of indigenous peoples, who used the waterways and riverbanks for their settlements for thousands of years.

As the Industrial Revolution developed in the United States, many enterprising industrialists looked to the Mississippi River as a promising source of water power. The combination of energy and easy access to river transportation attracted entrepreneurs and industrialists. In 1848, John Deere moved his plough business to Moline. His business was incorporated as Deere & Company in 1868 and is the largest employer today in the Quad Cities.

Champaign-Urbana

In 1974, I moved to the University of Illinois at Champaign-Urbana. These twin cities, founded in 1833, are home to the university. Champaign is the larger of the two cities. I discuss the university at some length later in this chapter.

It is useful to elaborate on the nature of "campus towns." These two cities are located in a sea of agricultural productivity, but the cultures revolve around the university and its 53,000 undergraduate and graduate students and 7,500 faculty and staff. The sports and cultural events and venues, all sponsored by the university, provide rich opportunities for interactions and celebrations.

I have had similar experiences at other Big Ten campus towns including Ann Arbor, MI (1824), Bloomington, IN (1818), Madison, WI (1836), and West Lafayette, IN (1836), although the Madison culture is also affected by being the state capital. The impacts of 50,000 young people are enormous.

During football Saturdays – for home games – campus towns are packed, with pubs and restaurants overflowing. Bands and cheerleaders liven the stadiums before games and at halftime. I repeatedly had the feeling that I was in the middle of a Walt Disney movie. Every home game day feels like the 4th of July. There was no comparable feeling in the Shining City, Gotham, or Capital.

Economic Base

I first encountered Illinois in 1973 when I flew into Champaign-Urbana to interview for a faculty position at the University of Illinois. Looking out the window as the airplane approached Willard Airport, I was mesmerized by the flat patchwork countryside of varying shades of green of what I soon learned were fields of corn and soybeans.

I had never experienced this scale of agricultural production. It was epitomized for me by Andersons Grain Elevator, northwest of the city. Eighteen wheelers full of grain would be lined up to unload. As each truck came to the head of the line, it was driven up a large ramp. The ramp was then tilted until the truck was almost vertical and its cargo flowed into underground cars that transported the grain to the elevators.

JOHN DEERE

Deere & Company began in 1836 when John Deere moved from Rutland, Vermont to Grand Detour, Illinois. Deere opened a shop in 1837, which enabled him to serve as a general repairman in the village, as well as a manufacturer of tools such as pitchforks and shovels. The item that set him apart was the self-scouring steel plow, when Deere fashioned a Scottish steel saw blade into a plow.

Prior to Deere's steel plow, most farmers used iron or wooden plows. The rich Midwestern soil stuck to these plows, so they had to be cleaned frequently. Deere created a highly polished steel surface that allowed the soil to slide easily. This addressed the difficulty of tilling Illinois' soil.

The traditional way of doing business was to make the product after it was ordered. Deere realized that this was not going to be a viable business model. Consequently, he increased the rate of manufacturing plows before putting them up for sale. This allowed customers to not only see what they were buying beforehand but also allowed his customers to purchase his products immediately.

Deere relocated to Moline, Illinois in 1848 to have access to the railroad and the Mississippi River. The company was manufacturing a variety of farm equipment products in addition to plows, such as wagons, corn planters, and cultivators.

Increased competition during the early 1900s from the new International Harvester Company led the company to expand its offerings in the implement business. The production of gasoline tractors came to define Deere & Company during the 20th century. The company produced its first combine harvester in 1927.

Deere & Company signed a definitive agreement to acquire Blue River Technology in 2017 to apply machine learning to agriculture. Blue River has designed and integrated computer vision and machine learning technology that will enable growers to reduce the use of herbicides by spraying only where weeds are present.

This scale was also reflected by the scope of the Illinois State Fair, held at the fairgrounds in Springfield each August. The Illinois State Fairgrounds encompasses over 360 acres of land with more than 150 buildings and over 1,000 stalls for livestock or horses. The Fair highlights ag-related industries, such as crops and animals, farm machinery manufacturing, and production and sale of value-added food products.

My only related experience was the Eastern States Exposition, an annual fair in West Springfield, Massachusetts, which is held for two weeks each September. All six New England states plus Delaware, New Jersey, New York, and Pennsylvania participate. While agriculture is highlighted, many other industries are well represented, reflecting the much more diverse economies of these ten states.

Illinois Agriculture

Illinois is a leading producer of soybeans, corn, and swine. The state's climate and varied soil types enable farmers to grow and raise many other agricultural commodities, including cattle, wheat, oats, sorghum, hay, sheep, poultry, fruits, and vegetables. As of 2019, Illinois had 72,000 farms covering 27 million acres – about 75% of the state's total land area. The average size of an Illinois farm is 375 acres. Most farm acreage is devoted to grain and legumes, mainly corn and soybeans.

Most of Illinois is comprised of fertile flat loess, left behind by glaciers and wind millions of years ago. Almost 90% of the state's cropland is considered prime farmland, ranking the state third nationally in total prime farmland acreage. Prime farmland is important because it provides an environmentally sound base for crop production. The central three-fourths of the state are especially well suited for growing crops, while hilly areas in the northwest and south provide excellent pasture for livestock.

Agriculture in the state of Illinois is big business. Illinois' agricultural commodities generate over $50 billion annually. Crops account for 40% of that total. Illinois ranks fifth nationally in the export of agricultural products with over $10 billion worth of goods shipped to other countries. Illinois is the nation's second leading exporter of both soybeans and feed grains. 274 million bushels of Illinois corn are annually used to produce more ethanol than any other state – about 678 million gallons. Illinois also markets other renewable fuels, including soybean-based biodiesel.

Billions of dollars flow into the state's economy from ag-related industries, such as farm vehicle and machinery manufacturing, agricultural real estate, and production and sale of value-added food products. With over 2,600 food manufacturing companies, Illinois is well-equipped to turn the state's crops and livestock into food and industrial products. The state ranks first in the nation with $180 billion in processed food sales. Most of these companies are located in the Chicago metropolitan area, which contains one of the largest concentrations of food-related businesses in the world. Upton Sinclair's 1906 book *The Jungle* exposed the practices of Chicago's meatpacking industry.

Illinois has a competitive edge over many other states due to its central location and superior transportation system. More than 2,000 miles of interstate highway and 34,500 miles of other state highways make trucking of goods fast and efficient. Chicago is home to the largest gateway in the nation, connecting the eastern and western United States. Illinois' 1,118 miles of navigable waterways, including the Illinois, Mississippi, and Ohio rivers, make barge traffic an excellent option for the shipment of grain to the Gulf of Mexico.

Illinois Economy

The Illinois GDP is $798 billion annually. As noted above, $230 billion is derived directly from agriculture and food processing. $120 billion comes from vehicles and equipment for agriculture and construction with Caterpillar ($59 billion), John Deere ($53 billion), and Navistar ($8 billion). Archer Daniels Midland adds $102 billion. So, over half the GDP directly revolves around agriculture.

Other major industries include insurance with Allstate ($45 billion) and State Farm ($79 billion) and pharma with Abbott ($44 billion), Baxter ($12 billion), and Walgreens ($22 billion). Transportation includes United Airlines ($45 billion) and automobile sales ($41 billion). Illinois is a much smaller player in automobile manufacturing than Michigan, Ohio, and Indiana.

It is easy to conclude that the Illinois economy, outside of metropolitan Chicago, is substantially driven by agriculture. Food production and processing, as well as vehicles and equipment, are the mainstays. This strongly influences the innovation outlook that I discuss at the end of this chapter.

Broader Context

To what extent is Illinois representative of the broader heartland of the United States? Of the top ten agricultural producing states in the United

States, Illinois, Indiana, Iowa, Kansas, Minnesota, Nebraska, and Wisconsin
are seven of the top 10. These states all border each other in the Midwest
and are similar geographically and culturally. Thus, it can easily be argued
that downstate Illinois is representative of the whole Heartland.

These seven states primarily produce grains and legumes for animal feed
and the breadbasket for humans. About 40% of the domestic corn crop and
over 60% of domestic soybeans are used to feed livestock. Thus, these
states play vital roles in the nation's food supply chain.

As an interesting aside, corn that is harvested when fully mature and dry
is considered a grain. It can be milled into cornmeal and used in such foods
as corn tortillas and cornbread. Popcorn is also harvested when it matures
and is considered to be a whole grain. Corn can also be a vegetable.
California, Florida, and Texas are primary US sources of fruits and vegetables.

Bodies of Water

The Heartland can be seen as endless vistas of fields of corn and soybeans.
Illinois, however, is laced with water resources. Lake Michigan is approximately 300 miles long and averages 75 miles across, covering 22,300 square
miles. It serves as the border between Illinois and Wisconsin on the west
and Michigan to the east.

The Mississippi River defines the western border of Illinois. For 216
miles, it serves as the border between Illinois and Iowa. Then for 327 miles
it defines the border between Illinois and Missouri. It plays a major role in
transporting agricultural products to the south.

The Ohio River defines the southern border of Illinois for 133 miles
between Illinois and Kentucky. The Illinois River flows for 273 miles from
metropolitan Chicago, southwest to the Mississippi River. Across these three
major rivers, there are 949 miles of navigable waterways.

Crossing Bodies of Water

There are 21 bridges between Illinois and Iowa and 29 bridges between
Illinois and Missouri, averaging roughly 10 miles between bridges across the
Mississippi River. There are six bridges between Illinois and Kentucky for
roughly 20 miles between bridges. Thirty-nine bridges cross the Illinois
River for approximately 7 miles between bridges.

The Lake Express Ferry crosses Lake Michigan four times daily during its spring and summer schedule. With the addition of evening sailings during its summer schedule, the Lake Express makes six Lake Michigan crossings daily during the height of the summer travel season. This ferry also provides service between Chicago and Milwaukee.

Higher Education

The University of Illinois at Champaign-Urbana is a member of the Big Ten Conference, the oldest Division I collegiate athletic conference in the United States. Founded as the Intercollegiate Conference of Faculty Representatives in 1896, it predates the founding of its regulating organization, the NCAA. For many decades, the conference consisted of 10 prominent universities but, as of 2014, it consists of 14 member institutions and 2 affiliate institutions, with 4 new member institutions scheduled to join in 2024.

Athletics receive substantial attention, but several member universities are stellar science and technology innovators. Illinois, Michigan, Northwestern, Purdue, and Wisconsin have top-ranked science and engineering programs. Illinois has numerous famous alumni and faculty members including the small sample:

- Marc Andreessen (1971), co-author of Mosaic and co-founder of Netscape; and co-founder and general partner of Silicon Valley venture capital firm
- John Bardeen (1908–1991), NAE, two Nobel Prizes in Physics for the transistor and superconductivity
- Arnold Beckman (1990–2004), NAE, Beckman Instruments CEO
- Donald Bitzer (1934), NAE, founder of PLATO
- Daniel Drucker (1918–2001), NAE, strength of materials
- Jack Kilby (1923–2005), NAE, Nobel Prize in Physics, inventor of integrated circuit
- Henry Petroski (1942–2023), NAE, wrote extensively about the design of buildings and bridges and how they failed. He also examined the history of commonplace objects like the pencil.
- James Reston (1909–1995), Pulitzer Prize, Executive Editor of *The New York Times*
- Jack Welch (1935–2020), NAE, General Electric CEO
- Rosalyn Yalow (1921–2011), Nobel Prize in Physiology or Medicine for development of the radioimmunoassay technique

I readily admit to bias in selecting this sample, tending to favor members of the National Academy of Engineering (NAE), of which I am a member, as well as scientists and engineers in general.

On the other hand, Illinois has been a very strong contributor to science and technology, particularly in computing. Thus, my sense is that Illinois' luminaries are disproportionally in science and technology, a fact I did not know when I joined the Illinois faculty, but soon came to very much appreciate.

Sports

Sports are a big deal in the Heartland. The Big Ten provides several highly regarded and watched rivalries. In football, the rivalry between Michigan and Ohio State is a classic. In basketball, Indiana and Michigan State have regularly provided highly ranked teams.

Professional sports in the Heartland also have many ardent fans. National Football League stalwarts include the Bears, Lions, Packers, and Vikings, and National Basketball Association teams include the Bucks, Bulls, Pacers, Pistons, and Timberwolves. Major League Baseball teams are the Brewers, Cardinals, Cubs, Tigers, Twins, and White Sox. National Hockey League teams include the Blackhawks, Blue Jackets, Blues, Redwings, and Wild.

Heartland Politics

Four US presidents were born in, or are claimed by, Illinois:

- Abraham Lincoln – 16th US President (1861–1865). Elected while Illinois resident
- Ulysses S. Grant – 18th US President (1869–1877). Elected while Illinois resident
- Ronald Reagan – 40th US President (1981–1989). Born in Tampico in 1911
- Barack Obama – 44th US President (2009–2017). Elected while Illinois resident

The city of Chicago and some of its older suburbs are heavily Democratic. This tendency has historically been balanced by Republican voters in the suburbs, although Democrats have significantly increased their suburban support in the past decade. Central Illinois' largely rural character helps to sustain a largely Republican voting pattern. Poorer soil, coal mining, and industrialization have caused the southern urbanized region around Saint Louis, Missouri, to lean Democratic.

Chicago Politics

In the 19th and early 20th centuries, Chicago sustained a strong two-party tradition that prevented the development of a centralized political machine. Neither the Democrats nor the Republicans succeeded in consolidating power citywide. Republicans prevailed most often in national elections; the Democrats won the majority of local contests.

Anton Cermak, a Bohemian immigrant of working-class origins, formed the potent Democratic machine that dominated Chicago politics for nearly half a century. Cermak secured control of the party hierarchy and won the 1931 mayoral campaign. He subsequently forced the party's dominant Irish contingent to accept other ethnic groups, bringing representatives from the German, Polish, Czech, and Jewish communities into leadership positions.

The life of the Democratic machine was cut short in 1933 when Cermak became the unintended victim of an attempted assassination of president-elect Franklin D. Roosevelt. After Cermak's death, the Irish seized control of the Democratic machine. Mayor Edward Kelly followed Cermak's practice of doling out patronage jobs, political appointments, and favors to a broad spectrum of ethnic groups.

He strengthened the political machine by utilizing three important sources. First, he became a fervent supporter of Franklin D. Roosevelt's New Deal and kept the city solvent through the liberal use of federal funds at a time when the Great Depression seriously threatened the financial well-being of municipal governments. Second, he acquired additional financial resources by ignoring the operation of gambling, prostitution, and other forms of vice, to obtain the funds necessary to keep the machine operating. Third, he actively cultivated African American voters, and his success paid huge dividends in later years when Chicago's black population increased dramatically.

Kelly repeatedly won reelection, but problems arose by the late 1940s. Concerns about the number of scandals in municipal government surfaced alongside a rising public outcry against the highly visible presence of organized crime in the city. Kelly's greatest liability proved to be his uncompromising stand in favor of public housing and desegregated public schools. The party leadership persuaded Kelly not to seek reelection.

Richard J. Daley was elected mayor in 1955. During Daley's 20+ years in city hall, the machine reached its apogee. At a time when virtually no urban political machines survived, Daley steered the Cook County Democratic organization to one electoral triumph after another. He controlled an estimated 35,000 patronage jobs, the use of which ensured party discipline and relegated the local Republican Party to insignificance.

Daley managed to circumvent civil service regulations by repeatedly hiring the same loyal Democrats to "temporary" jobs that were not subject to the regulations. As government workers died or retired, the machine filled their positions temporarily, pending civil service exams that were never given. Despite the conventional wisdom that political machines were hopelessly inefficient, Mayor Daley's reliable provision of services and apparent ability to balance the city's financial books led Chicago to be known as a city that works.

The election of Harold Washington as the city's first black mayor in 1983 and his subsequent reelection four years later unequivocally ended Democratic machine rule in Chicago. The election of mayor Richard M. Daley, the eldest son of the deceased boss, did not lead to resurrection of the machine in a new guise. As the younger Daley readily acknowledged, radically different demographics and the attendant alterations in the political calculus clearly made the machine politics for which Chicago became famous an anachronism by the end of the 20th century.

Abolitionist Era

Although Illinois' new Constitution of 1848 outlawed "slavery and involuntary servitude," slavery continued, but likely on a more limited basis. Records from the State Archives show the last recorded emancipation of an Illinois slave was in 1863, in the middle of the Civil War.

Near the close of the Civil War, Illinois repealed the anti-Black law and became the first state to ratify the Thirteenth Amendment to the Constitution of the United States, which abolished slavery nationally.

John and Mary Jones were significant figures in the abolitionist movement in the early history of Chicago. John Jones was the undisputed leader of Chicago's emerging black community from the 1850s through the 1870s, rising to national prominence as an abolitionist and an early civil rights leader.

Progressive Era

The Progressive Era was a bottom-up response to the Gilded Age when robber barons exploited society for profits while avoiding accountability for the financial, physical, and psychological consequences of their greed. President Theodore Roosevelt was a leader among those trying to redress grievances.

Upton Sinclair wrote *The Jungle*, published in 1906, to expose the appalling working conditions in the meatpacking industry, focused on Chicago. His description of diseased, rotten, and contaminated meat shocked the public and led to new federal food safety laws. Before the turn of the 20th century, a major reform movement had emerged in the United States.

Civil Rights Era

Founded in 1942 by an interracial group of students in Chicago, the Congress of Racial Equality (CORE) pioneered the use of nonviolent direct action in America's civil rights struggle. CORE played a major role in the civil rights era.

The Chicago Freedom Movement was the most ambitious civil rights campaign in the North of the United States. It lasted from mid-1965 to August 1966 and is largely credited with inspiring the 1968 Fair Housing Act. These two endeavors highlight Illinois' legacy of supporting disadvantaged populations.

Challenges

All ecosystems have economic, political, and environmental challenges, but the nature of these challenges tends to differ based on the characteristics of the ecosystem.

Economic Challenges

During the last few decades, there has been a significant decline in the number of farms. Along with this decline, there has been a trend in farm consolidation which has increased the average size of farms. There are likely economic benefits to this for the remaining farm enterprises, but it does increase uncertainty about the future of entry-level farming.

Technology trends and the costs of advanced technologies also affect the abilities of small farmers to compete.

Political Challenges

There is a portfolio of national, state, and local government policies. These policies may influence what a farmer grows, where a farm is located, how products are transported and processed, how a commodity is traded, and the price the farmer might receive. This can create uncertainty amidst the environmental challenges discussed below.

Large farm corporations can more easily afford the large campaign contributions that grease the American political system. Thus, small farmers have difficulty gaining political support for measures that would protect them.

Environmental Challenges

Illinois' agricultural operations unfortunately often lead to the contamination of water resources. Damages include soil erosion, which leads to sedimentation in waterways; nutrient pollution from phosphorus and nitrogen contained in fertilizer and animal manure; and pesticide pollution. Regulations regarding these phenomena are likely to become stricter. At the very least, this will increase the costs of operations.

Global warming and climate change may require farmers to switch crops to those more well-suited to changing weather and environmental threats. Weeds, pests, and diseases are expected to increase because of warmer winters, increased spring precipitation, and higher temperatures. This will have significant negative effects on crops and livestock in Illinois.

Innovation Outlook

Ability to address the above challenges requires scale. The large players in the Heartland understand this. The growth opportunities discussed below provide the rationale for this approach to pursuing innovation.

Venture Capital Funding

In 2020, the Illinois venture capital ecosystem closed 151 venture deals for a total of $2.9 billion invested. This represents a 74% increase over the amount invested in the State the previous year. However, this is modest compared to Massachusetts, a state with comparable GDP.

This should perhaps be expected. The large players in the agricultural sector – Archer Daniels Midland, Caterpillar, and Deere – do not tend to rely on venture capital. The growth opportunities discussed next require major investments, not venture capital seeding.

Growth Opportunities

Illinois, considered broadly, likely has growth opportunities in insurance, pharma, and transportation. However, the opportunities in the Heartland necessarily focus on agriculture. The confluence of the above challenges and technology trends suggests significant opportunities for innovation.

Precision agriculture involves sensing crop conditions and optimizing planting, fertilization, and cultivation. This is a key component of the third wave of modern agricultural revolutions. The first agricultural revolution was the increase of mechanized agriculture, from 1900 to 1930. Each farmer produced enough food to feed about 25 or so people during this time. The 1960s prompted the Green Revolution with new methods of genetic modification, which led to each farmer feeding over 150 people.

It is expected that by 2050, the global population will approach 10 billion, and food production must effectively double from current levels in order to feed every mouth. With new technological advancements in the agricultural revolution of precision farming, each farmer should be able to feed 265 people on the same acreage. Companies such as Archer Daniels Midland and Deere are key players in this quest.

Precision agriculture is a farm management strategy based on observing, measuring, and responding to temporal and spatial variability to improve the sustainability of agricultural production. It is used in both crop and livestock production. Precision agriculture often employs technologies to automate agricultural operations, improving their diagnoses, decision-making, or performance. Conceptual work on precision agriculture and practical applications began in the late 1980s.

The goal of precision agriculture research is to define a decision support system for whole farm management with the goal of optimizing returns on inputs while preserving resources. Beyond productivity, precision agriculture can support responding to the challenges outlined earlier. Managing environmental impacts can also be central.

Table 4.1   Innovation Assessment for Heartland

	Innovation Outlook			
	Precision Agriculture	*Insurance Products*	*Pharma Offerings*	*Transportation Services*
Strengths	Incumbency Reputation	Incumbency Installed Base	Incumbency Installed Base	Incumbency Installed Base
Weaknesses	High Taxes & Labor Costs	High Taxes & Labor Costs	High Taxes & Labor Costs	High Taxes & Labor Costs
Opportunities	Sell Expertise Globally	Expanded Product Lines	Expand Supply Chain Partners	Intermodal Integration
Threats	Low-Cost Providers	Global Competition	Global Competition	Global Competition

Innovation Assessment

Table 4.1 summarizes the strengths, weaknesses, opportunities, and threats for each growth opportunity of the innovation outlook for Heartland. Clearly, this ecosystem is in a very strong position in agriculture in terms of incumbency, reputation, and very long track records of success. The other opportunities are very attractive but the ecosystem's position is not as dominant in these areas. The main overarching challenge is high taxes and labor costs, which provides opportunities for lower-cost competitors to take market shares.

There are interesting opportunities for Heartland. They can market and sell agricultural expertise globally. Within insurance, expansions of product lines seem warranted, perhaps in terms of uncertainties and risks associated with precision agriculture. Pharma might invest in expanded supply chains. Transportation should emphasize intermodal opportunities, perhaps with an emphasis on agricultural products.

Epilogue

How do the Heartland and Shining City ecosystems compare? The University of Illinois has 44,000 undergraduate students while MIT has 11,000. Illinois is in a rural setting, while MIT is in a bustling urban setting. Yet both MIT and Illinois are top five schools of engineering, so the quality of faculty and students are comparable.

The major difference for me was that MIT feels like a major player in a diverse ecosystem of academia, government, and industry, while Illinois feels like it is the ecosystem. Both institutions ambitiously pursue excellence, but the pace and the complexity feel much greater in Cambridge than in Urbana.

Yet, Heartland's agricultural dominance cannot be replaced like Shining City's relatively brief enjoyment of dominating mini-computers. Agriculture totally depends on geography; computing does not. This dependency includes fertile soil, but also bodies of water that enable expeditious transport of the bulk inputs and outputs of agricultural production.

Thus, innovation ecosystems emerge as designs tailored to the affordances and hindrances provided by the characteristics of their environments. No two of the eight ecosystems in this book are identical. This inherent diversity is a strength of the overall portfolio of ecosystems. Cookie cutter ecosystems are not a good idea.

In Chapter 10, I compare and contrast the innovation assessments for the eight ecosystems. There are, of course, some elements in common, but there are also significant differences. Such differences, when well understood, can provide a basis for sustainable competitive advantages.

Overall, a central goal should be the creation of competitive advantages that are sustainable. This can be achieved by capabilities that cannot be easily copied, for example, Heartland's soil and rivers, or by abilities to adapt to change quickly, a strong suit of Silicon Valley, for instance. A key insight to be gained is the extent to which one is more dependent on the former or the latter.

Chapter 5

Old Country

Chapters 2–4 all involved ecosystems in the United States. This chapter addresses the ecosystem of the Netherlands, with a few excursions more broadly. The Pilgrims, discussed in Chapter 3, departed in 1620 from Delfs Haven, Holland, for North America. They first sailed to Southampton, England, to join the Mayflower, which was also making the voyage. After leaks forced the Speedwell to make additional stops in Dartmouth and then Plymouth, its passengers boarded the Mayflower. Five months later the Pilgrims settled the Plymouth Colony in present-day Massachusetts.

Pre-settlement

The prehistory of the Netherlands was heavily influenced by the region's constantly changing, low-lying geography. Inhabited by humans for at least 37,000 years, the landscape underwent significant transformations, from the last ice age's tundra climate to the emergence of various Paleolithic and Mesolithic groups. The region witnessed the development of a culture, closely linked to rivers and open water. The arrival of agriculture around 5000–4000 BC marked the beginning of a new culture, which gradually transformed prehistoric communities.

A succession of cultural groups left their mark on the area. The Bronze Age heralded increased prosperity and trade, with the construction of notable monuments such as the dolmens in Drenthe. The Iron Age brought about the spread of Germanic and Celtic influences. The pre-Roman period was characterized by a complex interplay of different cultures and ethnicities.

DOI: 10.4324/9781003507468-5

For 450 years, from around 55 BC to AD 410, the southern part of the Netherlands was integrated into the Roman Empire. The Rhine River marked the northern boundary of the empire and formed the oldest section of the Roman lines. The Roman period in the Netherlands began in the year 19 BC, when two or three legions established a camp in Nijmegen.

Founding

Charlemagne (747–814) united most of Western Europe for the first time since the classical era of the Roman Empire, as well as uniting parts of Europe that had never been under French or Roman rule. Holland emerged as a named entity around 1083, soon enough to play a role in the Crusades. There were eight major Crusade expeditions occurring between 1096 and 1291.

The Duke of Burgundy united the Netherlands and Belgium in 1433. William I, Prince of Orange, also known as William the Silent or more commonly known as William of Orange, led the Dutch Revolt against the Spanish Habsburgs, which sparked the Eighty Years' War and eventually gained formal independence of the United Provinces in 1581.

The internal peace of the republic was secured by the conclusion of the general peace of Westphalia, signed in October of 1648. This treaty has long been considered not only as the fundamental law of the empire but also as the basis of the political system of Europe.

The Dutch Golden Age roughly spanned the era from 1588 to 1672, in which Dutch trade, science, and art as well as the Dutch military were among the most acclaimed in the world. This period included the Eighty Years' War, which ended in 1648.

Napoleon decided to make Holland an integral part of France in 1810. After annexing the southern provinces of Holland into the Empire, he subsequently annexed the rest of the kingdom into the French Empire. The Battle of Waterloo was fought in June 1815 between Napoleon's French Army and a coalition led by the Duke of Wellington. The loss ended French attempts to dominate Europe.

Consequently, the Napoleonic Kingdom of Holland was short-lived. Nevertheless, in the aftermath of Napoleon's fall, the precedent of the Netherlands having been a Kingdom facilitated the House of Orange's successful efforts to upgrade themselves to being fully-fledged monarchs.

In contrast to my depiction of earlier settlers in Chapters 2–4, the origin of the Netherlands was dominated by emperors, kings, queens, dukes, counts, and bishops. The controversies, conflicts, and realignments were endless. It would be a long time until democracy had a chance in the late 18th century and continues to be challenged even today.

It is interesting to briefly consider the Normans. The North Men were renegades and plunderers from Denmark, Norway, and Sweden who played central roles. French King Charles III ceded the territory around Rouen and the mouth of the Seine River to Rollo, the chief of the largest band of Vikings, in the Treaty of aint-Clair-sur-Epte in 911. This became the Duchy of Normandy. William the Conqueror led the Norman invasion of England in 1066. Consequently, Normandy and England were linked for almost 150 years by having the same person reign as both Duke of Normandy and King of England.

I include this tangent because my mother's family, originating in Perci in Normandy, joined the Norman invasion. They settled in Northumberland near the border with Scotland. The family built and still owns Alnwick Castle, the venue for Hogwarts in the Harry Potter movies. My discovery of this linkage provided great pleasure to my family.

Cities and Towns

The country is divided into 11 provinces – North and South Holland, Zealand, North Brabant, Utrecht, Limburg, Gelderland, Overyssel, Drenthe, Groningen, and Friesland. There are three large rivers – the Rhine, the Meuse, and the Scheldt. The inhabitants are Low Germans (Dutch), French, Saxon, Frisian, and Jews. The leading religion of the country is Lutheran, but there are also many Catholics and persons of other faiths, all of whom are permitted the enjoyment of their creeds.

Amsterdam is both the capital and the largest city with a population of over 800,000. Rotterdam is second largest with a population exceeding 600,000. Amsterdam is known for over 60 miles of canals, about 90 islands, and 1,500 bridges. Southwest of Amsterdam, about 30 minutes away, is Keukenhof, arguably the global flower capital. Rotterdam is 1 hour south and the largest port in the European Union.

The Hague is also only 1 hour south. West of The Hague is Scheveningen, a North Sea beach resort. East of The Hague is Delft where I lived for a year in 1979–1980. It amazed this American that the New Church was built in 1496 and the Old Church in 1246. It struck me that this really was the old country.

Not having a car, the excellent public transportation system was wonderful. We walked the 63 miles along the North Sea from Den Helder in the north to Hook of Holland in the south in five days, going home to Delft between each leg of the hike. Trips from Delft included Rotterdam by train in 1 hour and Amsterdam by train in 1.5 hours.

Longer jaunts included Paris by train for 3.5 hours to enjoy the Paris Opera. London involved a 6.5-hour ferry trip from Hook of Holland to Harwich plus some time on trains from either end to enjoy museums and plays in London. The train trip to Berlin was 8 hours to enjoy the Berlin Philharmonic Orchestra conducted by Herbert von Karajan.

Cultural, social, and political history and contemporary ongoings were readily accessible without taking any flights and not even involving automobiles. Such easy access is very difficult in the United States, but not impossible as the chapters on the next three innovation ecosystems illustrate. Access to, ease of use, and costs of mobility are important elements of an innovation ecosystem.

Economic Base

The Netherlands' annual GDP is over $1 trillion. In contrast, the US GDP is $24 trillion, and the largest state, California, has just under $4 trillion. World GDP is $97 trillion. However, keep in mind that the Netherlands is a bit smaller than Maryland.

The stage was set for their success with the formation of the Dutch East India Company. The United East India Company was a chartered company established in March 1602 by the States General of the Netherlands, amalgamating existing companies into the first joint-stock company in the world. The value of its stock reached a staggering $8.3 trillion in 1637. It ceased operations in 1799.

Thus, the Dutch have been global players for over four centuries. The biggest enterprises are Royal Dutch Shell with $381 billion in annual revenues, although they moved their headquarters to the UK in 2022. Stellantis is second with $191 billion in annual revenue resulting from the merger of Fiat Chrysler and PSA Group (Citroen, Peugeot) in 2021. Renault remains with Nissan.

Other significant contributors to GDP include Ahold ($94 billion), tourism ($92 billion), Unilever ($64 billion), agriculture ($53 billion), ING ($47 billion), Royal Philips ($20 billion), shipping ($9 billion), and flowers ($5 billion). Thus, the Dutch economy is highly diversified and resilient.

ROYAL DUTCH SHELL

Royal Dutch Shell was formed in 1907 through the merger of the Royal Dutch Petroleum Company of the Netherlands and the "Shell" Transport and Trading Company of the United Kingdom. According to the company website, the origin of the Shell name can be traced back to the seashells that Marcus Samuel senior imported from the Far East during the late 19th century. When his sons Marcus junior and Samuel were looking for a name for the kerosene that they were exporting to Asia, they chose Shell. The combined company rapidly became the leading competitor of John D. Rockefeller's American Standard Oil. By 1920, Shell was the largest producer of oil in the world. Shell was one of the "Seven Sisters" which dominated the global petroleum industry from the mid-1940s to the mid-1970s. In recent decades, gas has become an increasingly important part of Shell's business and Shell acquired BG Group in 2016. Shell was the ninth-largest corporate producer of greenhouse gas emissions in the period 1988–2015. Shell is the second-largest investor-owned oil company in the world (after ExxonMobil), the largest company headquartered in the United Kingdom, the second-largest company headquartered in Europe (after Volkswagen), and the 15th largest company in the world.

Main exports are machinery and transport equipment (28 percent of total exports), mineral fuels (23 percent), food (11 percent), clothing and footwear (10 percent), and pharmaceuticals (5 percent). Over 60 percent of total exports are sent to European Union countries.

The Netherlands produces 1.7 billion cut flowers per year, which represents roughly 60 percent of global trade in flowers and makes it the Silicon Valley of the flower industry. The Netherlands ranks first in the European Union in terms of agricultural exports and ranks second in the world, after the United States. Some of the food and agricultural products exported by the Netherlands include tomatoes, chilies, cucumbers, apples, flowers, flower bulbs, and fresh-cut plants. The foodstuffs industry is one of the country's biggest industries.

Other major industries include energy, chemicals, trade, machinery, metallurgy, electrical goods and services, and tourism. The energy industry in the Netherlands is one of the country's key exports and serves as a source of national income. It is estimated that 25 percent of all natural gas reserves in the European Union (EU) are located in the Netherlands. Large natural gas deposits were discovered in the Netherlands in 1959 and have generated significant revenues for decades.

The chemical industry of the Netherlands is one of the country's leading economic sectors. The country contains the headquarters of 19 of the world's leading multinational chemical companies, including Royal Dutch Shell, DSM, AkzoNobel, and BASF. The Netherlands is also home to research institutions such as the Netherlands Organization for Applied Scientific Research (TNO) and numerous universities. I worked closely with TNO during my year at Delft, focused on studies of supertanker operations.

The Netherlands is a leading supplier of chemical products and services, and the extensive transport network in the Netherlands makes raw materials easily accessible. Its chemical industry focuses on developing smart materials and solutions in five areas: healthcare, energy, food security, climate and resources, and transport. The industry also works across many sectors, bringing together various stakeholders to develop smart materials and new solutions.

The metallurgy industry is an important part of the manufacturing sector in the Netherlands. The industry is made up of different components, such as equipment, services, consumables, and software. The metallurgy industry in the Netherlands is highly dependent upon both traditional craftsmanship and modern techniques of production. The industry works together with other sectors such as energy and power, healthcare, mining, automobile, real estate, and private shipbuilding. Examples of key companies in the country's metallurgy industry include Kapco, Hindustan Machine Tools, DMG Mori, Colfax, BTD Manufacturing, Atlas Copco, and Amada.

The Netherlands is among the world's top 20 largest steel exporters. In 2017, the Netherlands exported 11.3 million metric tons of steel, and in 2016, the country accounted for 2 percent of all global steel exports. The Netherlands exports steel to more than 160 countries and territories.

Broader Contexts

Does my immersion in the Netherlands provide broader insights into European Union innovation ecosystems? My year living there provided a wealth of EU country experiences in Denmark, Finland, Germany, and Sweden. I have also had decades-long experiences across most and perhaps all EU countries.

Denmark, Finland, Norway, and Sweden, and sometimes Iceland and the Netherlands, are often characterized as socialist democracies. However, each of these countries has its own economic and political model – termed a mixed model – which bears hallmarks of both socialism and capitalism. Thus, we cannot simply bin countries as socialist and capitalist.

I did find their approach to higher education, in general, rather different than the United States. Higher education is much more centrally funded. Faculty are not as incentivized to seek and gain external resources. Top positions are very constrained; few people become full professors. Tenure in the sense of "up or out" is not practiced. One can remain a member of the non-senior faculty for one's whole career.

As I later discuss, business is much more regulated; for example, the hiring and firing of employees is constrained. Taxation is much more significant. Business formation is secondary to employment security. The opportunities to become enormously wealthy are much less than in the United States, for better or worse.

Bodies of Water

The North Sea is the western border of the country. There are three major rivers flowing west to east into the North Sea. The Rhine River (766 miles) flows from two small headways in the Alps of east-central Switzerland north and west through Rotterdam to the sea.

The Meuse River (575 miles) forms the Belgian-Dutch border. The Scheldt River (224 miles) flows through northern France, western Belgium, and the southwestern part of the Netherlands, with its mouth at the North Sea. The Rhine–Meuse–Scheldt delta, with almost 10,000 square miles, is the largest river delta in Europe.

Crossing Bodies of Water

The number of bridges crossing the three rivers is too high to enumerate. Amsterdam, the capital of the Netherlands, as noted earlier, has more than 62 miles of canals, about 90 islands, and 1,500 bridges. Crossing water is a frequent Dutch experience.

Crossing the North Sea to England involves private boats, a ferry from the Hook of Holland to Harwich, or the Chunnel. The Channel Tunnel is a

30-plus-mile underwater railway tunnel that connects Folkestone, UK, with Coquelles, France beneath the English Channel at the Strait of Dover. It is the only fixed link between the island of Great Britain and the European mainland. Of course, one can also fly.

Higher Education

All the major universities in the Netherlands are public institutions supported by the state. They are not free but are highly subsidized.

The Dutch equivalents of the Ivy League in the United States include Leiden University (1575), University of Groningen (1614), University of Amsterdam (1632), Utrecht University (1636), and Erasmus University (1913). In contrast, Harvard was founded in 1636, Yale in 1701, and Princeton in 1746.

Technology-centered institutions came a couple of centuries later, including Delft University of Technology (1842), Eindhoven University of Technology (1956), and Twente University (1961). MIT in the United States was founded in 1861 and Stanford University in 1885.

I served as a professor of mechanical engineering at Delft for the year of 1979–1980. Having graduated from MIT, I found engineering at Delft to be similarly excellent to MIT. It was a very positive experience, both professionally and personally.

Politics

The present government is a hereditary monarchy, consisting of a king or queen and States General, with 150 members of the House of Representatives and 75 Senators. Dutch politics and governance reflect a common striving for broad consensus on important issues, within both the political community and society as a whole.

The States General currently includes members of 15 political parties. The three largest parties are:

■ The People's Party for Freedom and Democracy (VVD) is a conservative liberal party. It has more sympathy for private enterprise and economic freedom compared to other Dutch parties.

- Democrats 66 (D66) is a center to center-left social liberal party. The party supports liberal policies on social issues such as abortion, drugs, and euthanasia and stands for human rights and LGBT progress. D66 is also a strong supporter of European integration.
- The Party for Freedom (PVV) is a nationalist conservative, right popu- listic, and anti-Islam party. Its philosophy is based on maintaining the integrity of Dutch culture, and opposition to immigration and European integration. It is mostly economically liberal.

On polling day, all Dutch nationals aged 18 or over may cast their vote for a candidate on the candidate list. By casting their vote, people make known which party they want to gain seats in Parliament and perhaps also in the Cabinet. The Netherlands' multi-party system usually leads to no one party ever securing an overall majority of votes, so several parties must cooperate to form a coalition government.

The Netherlands is a member of the EU and the North Atlantic Treaty Organization (NATO).

Abolitionist Era

The Dutch participated in the transatlantic slave trade. Dutch slave traders shipped around 600,000 enslaved Africans to the New World, which is roughly 5 percent of the total of the transatlantic slave trade. In 1863 slavery was abolished in all Dutch colonies. Dutch King Willem-Alexander, com- memorating the anniversary of the abolition of slavery in 2023, apologized for the Netherlands' historic involvement in slavery and the effects that it still has today.

Progressive Era

Progressive reform across the globe helped lay the foundations of modern public administration and social welfare systems in America and Western Europe. The American Progressive Era and the progressive reforms shaped European welfare states. Public administrators adopted new bureaucratic methods and processes to carry out their functions and mandates. These new administrative processes were rooted in principles and methods associ- ated with the Gilded Age and the scientific revolution.

Civil Rights Era

In comparison to the civil rights movement in the United States, Europe's history of anti-racism activism is short. Despite a number of large-scale protest movements, civil rights issues and concerns have yet to break into the European mainstream or force lasting political change. This may reflect the relatively less pronounced use of slave labor compared to the southern United States, as well as the mass suppression of indigenous people throughout the United States.

Challenges

All ecosystems have economic, political, and environmental challenges, but the nature of these challenges tends to differ based on the characteristics of the ecosystem.

Economic Challenges

Inflation is still high and investment in badly needed housing is cooling. Worker productivity is experiencing low growth, in part because capital investment per worker is declining.

The labor market is tight, partially due to the working age population declining. Increased immigration is needed to grow the workforce, although immigrants pose challenges as well – see below. Increased affordable childcare is needed to attract more people to work.

Much greater investment is needed in training. This, in turn, requires investments to attract and retain teachers. All of the innovation growth opportunities discussed below require highly skilled workforces.

Political Challenges

After 18 months in power, the Dutch four-party coalition government collapsed over bitter migration policy disputes. For months, Dutch Prime Minister Mark Rutte tried to negotiate a package of measures to reduce the flow of new migrants arriving in the Netherlands.

A related challenge is the very slow assimilation of non-western immigrants in terms of achieving income parity with Western immigrants and natives. Non-Western immigrants tend to congregate in low-prosperity enclaves of similar immigrants.

Environmental Challenges

The North Sea's waters have long presented enormous environmental challenges due to recurrent flooding. Sea level rise from global warming will exacerbate these challenges. Fortunately, the Dutch have the expertise and commitment to meet such challenges.

The pursuit of low-carbon energy is a top priority. They need to more aggressively pursue their goals in this area. It is all too easy to lose track of the long term when near-term challenges seem overwhelming.

Innovation Outlook

Venture Capital Funding

Since the financial crisis, Dutch VC funds have managed over $30 billion per year. Almost 50 percent of these investments came from outside the Netherlands. This indicates that VC investors from abroad are interested and active in investing in Dutch ventures.

Growth Opportunities

The Netherlands has a long history of technological innovations, ranging from the microscope, telescope, and submarines to cyber security, AI, and digital health. They have fostered strong crossovers between tech and other high impact industries, such as smart farming and agtech, robotics, smart mobility, and sustainable energy and chemicals.

The Netherlands has an international reputation for innovative water management, creating integrated and inclusive solutions that protect people and infrastructure from flooding, prevent water scarcity, and ensure supplies of clean and safe water. Other countries look to the Netherlands for expertise in these areas.

The Netherlands is one of the world's largest agricultural producers, exporting $69 billion worth of vegetables, fruit, flowers, meat and dairy products each year. In terms of Dutch agriculture, the sector produces mostly cereals (wheat in particular), feed crops (such as fodder maize), and potatoes.

The Dutch have pioneered cell-cultured meat, vertical farming, seed technology, and robotics in milking and harvesting. They have also spearheaded innovations that focus on decreased water usage as well as reduced carbon and methane emissions associated with agriculture.

The Netherlands is aiming for a rapid transition to a low-carbon economy and has placed ambitious greenhouse gas (GHG) reduction targets at the center of energy and climate policy. The 2019 Climate Act sets targets for reducing GHG emissions by 49 percent by 2030 and by 95 percent by 2050 (versus 1990 levels). The Netherlands is pioneering green hydrogen, battery, and smart-grid energy technologies.

Innovation Assessment

Table 5.1 summarizes the strengths, weaknesses, opportunities, and threats for each growth opportunity of the innovation outlook for Old Country. Clearly, this ecosystem is in a very strong position in terms of incumbency, reputation, and very long track records of success. The main challenge is high taxes and labor costs, which provides opportunities for low-cost competitors to nibble at market shares.

The Dutch have long been internationalists. Other countries look to them for expertise in smart supply chains, water management, and precision agriculture, where they already have strong positions and reputations. Success in low-carbon energy will likely require partnerships across the EU, an inclination the Dutch have long been refining. There are strong competitive threats in all of these growth areas, but the Dutch have centuries of experiences in such competitions.

Table 5.1 Innovation Assessment for Old Country

	Innovation Outlook			
	Smart Supply Chains	*Water Management*	*Precision Agriculture*	*Low-Carbon Energy*
Strengths	Incumbency Water Access	Incumbency Reputation	Incumbency Market Position	Commitment Investments
Weaknesses	High Taxes & Labor Costs	High Taxes & Labor Costs	High Taxes & Labor Costs	High Taxes & Labor Costs
Opportunities	Sell Expertise Globally	Sell Expertise Globally	Sell Expertise Globally	Broad EU Partnerships
Threats	Modes Other Than Water	Global Consultants	Low-Cost Competitors	Global Competition

Epilogue

Our year in the Netherlands was thoroughly enjoyable and highly educational. With great public transportation, we avoided having a car, yet traveled all over Western Europe. We bought groceries every day when walking home from work at the University. We developed our now long-held habits of pubs and wine bars in Delft. We passed our required Dutch classes but rarely spoke other than English.

It is interesting to contrast EU social welfare states such as Holland to the US market economy. Total taxation in the United States, including federal, state, and local taxes on incomes sales, and property amounts to roughly 26 percent of GDP in the United States. In Scandinavia and the Netherlands, these taxes amount to 45 percent. For this dramatic increase in taxes, one pays nothing for healthcare, education, or retirement, and everyone receives the same levels of services. Equity is assured.

Thus, the EU seems to be a better place to live for people in general. However, it may be that the United States is a better place to launch and operate a business. Roughly halfway through our stay in Holland, we formed a US company, Search Technology, Inc., to design, develop, and sell professional training simulators. I decided to explore how we might have launched this company in the Netherlands, mainly as an interesting exercise rather than a serious intention.

This would have been much more complicated with many more regulatory processes in the EU. In particular, long-term commitments to employees were much more substantial. For instance, if sales turned south in the United States, one could not simply lay off employees. You were required to keep paying employees in the EU despite a lack of sales and revenues to pay them. This would add a significant risk management component to hiring plans.

Consequently, in the EU hiring employees involves a much bigger commitment and sufficient reserves to address possible shortfalls. At the very least, this delays or retards business formation. This may explain in part why there are no "big tech" companies in the EU like Amazon, Apple, Google, and Microsoft. Would-be EU entrepreneurs are effectively forced to be more risk averse.

Innovation ecosystems may vary in levels of risk-taking for cultural and social reasons. But variations can also be affected by legal, political, and economic forces. Space does not allow for elaborating on some of my other experiences, example, in Africa. However, pushback from would-be entrepreneurs who see opportunities as much too risky has been a frequent experience.

Entrepreneurs in the United States may be naively risk seeking. They do not believe the overall failure probabilities apply to them. There is often a sense that failure is just an opportunity to pick yourself up and try again. The failure rate is very high, but initial capitalization can be modest because employees in the United States are not protected from failure.

The result is higher rates of business formation, but greater economic disruption as ill-conceived businesses fail and employees must seek new employment. Younger employees, at least in the United States, seem to accept these risks and simply move on to new opportunities. This form of resilience seems much less common outside the United States. Of course, there is a pervasive sense in the United States that everyone can eventually be a business owner.

Chapter 6

New South

In the 1960s, in an effort to promote Atlanta as a racially progressive city and to distinguish Atlanta from the racial violence occurring in other Southern cities, city leaders coined the moniker "The City Too Busy Too Hate." Belying this marketing slogan were the deeply embedded segregation laws, policies, and practices that restricted all aspects of African Americans' lives. Despite these barriers, African Americans were making progress, but always within the constraints of racial inequality.

The traditional color line in housing, education, and politics in Atlanta soon began to crumble as African Americans asserted their increasing political power and the civil rights movement began to focus attention and energy on the overthrow of Jim Crow. It also accelerated the exodus of white Atlantans to the suburbs.

During the 1960s the white population of the city declined by 60,132, while the black population increased by 68,587. The 1970 census revealed that Atlanta had a majority black population for the first time in the city's history. Maynard Jackson Jr. was Atlanta's first African American mayor; he served two consecutive terms (1974–1978; 1978–1982) and served a third term in 1990–1994. Andrew Young was mayor between Jackson's second and third terms.

Over the last several years, Atlanta has garnered a reputation as one of the country's fastest-growing and most prolific technology hubs. Forbes Magazine named the metro area as one of the world's elite tech towns, placing it in the number three spot of cities poised to become tech meccas in the near future. It is clearly an innovative ecosystem.

DOI: 10.4324/9781003507468-6

Colonial Founding

Europeans vied for control of Georgia in the early 1700s. Spain claimed it as part of its Florida territory and England as part of its Carolina territory. In 1733, British military leader James Oglethorpe established the last of the 13 original British colonies, Georgia, named after King George II.

Georgia's settlers cleared the land, built houses, and constructed fortifications. Those who came in the first wave of settlement soon realized that royal support was limited and they were on their own. Oglethorpe, who went to Georgia with the first settlers, began negotiating treaties with local Indian tribes, especially the Upper Creek tribe.

Knowing that the Spanish, based in Florida, had great influence with many of the tribes in the region, Oglethorpe thought it necessary to reach an understanding with these native peoples if Georgia was to remain free from attack. In addition, the Indian trade became an important element of Georgia's economy.

John Wesley and his brother Charles arrived in Savannah in 1735. Wesley went to the colony to evangelize the Native Americans but ended up spending most of his ministry preaching to European settlers as a church pastor in Savannah. Wesley founded Methodism, a movement that sought to reform the Church of England from within. It became separate from its parent body and developed into an autonomous denomination.

Founding of Atlanta

In 1836, Georgia decided to build a railroad to the US Midwest and a location was chosen to be the line's terminus. The stake marking the founding of "Terminus" was driven into the ground at the Zero Mile Post in 1837. By 1839, homes and a store had been built and the settlement grew. Between 1845 and 1854, rail lines arrived from four different directions, and the rapidly growing town quickly became the rail hub for the entire Southern United States.

The town was first named Marthasville in honor of the then-governor's daughter, nicknamed Terminus for its rail location, and then soon changed to Atlanta, the feminine of Atlantic, relating to the Western and Atlantic, the founding railroad line.

During the American Civil War, the distribution hub of Atlanta became the target of a major Union campaign. In 1864, Union General William

Sherman's troops set on fire and destroyed the city's assets and buildings, save churches and hospitals. The population grew rapidly after the war, as did manufacturing, while the city retained its role as a rail hub.

Coca-Cola was launched by Asa Candler in 1886 and grew into an Atlanta-based world empire. Electric streetcars arrived in 1889, and the city extended service to the expanding suburbs. Grant Park was founded in 1883. Inman Park was the first planned suburb in 1889. Druid Hills followed in 1893.

Economic Base

World War II prompted strong industrial and business growth in Atlanta. It continued and accelerated during the postwar years. In 1947 a new Ford automobile assembly plant was opened in Hapeville. General Motors opened a new factory in Doraville the following year. Bell Aircraft, the city's biggest wartime employer, scaled down substantially following the war. The Marietta facility reopened as Lockheed-Georgia in early 1951. By 1954 there were hundreds of new industries in Atlanta and almost 1,200 national corporations with offices in the city.

The current GDP of metro Atlanta exceeds $400 billion. Major corporations with headquarters in Atlanta include:

- Chick-fil-A
- Children's Healthcare of Atlanta
- Coca-Cola
- Cox Communications
- Delta Air Lines
- Emory Health
- Equifax
- Genuine Parts
- Georgia Pacific
- Georgia Power
- Home Depot
- NCR
- Newell Brands
- Northside Hospital
- Piedmont Atlanta
- Southern Company

- Truist Banks
- Wellstar Health System

Five of these 18 corporations are health systems. Emory, Northside, and Piedmont are three of the top five employers in Atlanta, the other two being Delta Air Lines and Home Depot. Health continues to be very labor intensive, but technology trends discussed later may mitigate this situation.

COCA-COLA

Coca-Cola was originally marketed as an alcohol-free drink and intended as a patent medicine. It was invented in the late 19th century by Dr. John Pemberton, who introduced it at Jacobs' Pharmacy in downtown Atlanta on May 8, 1886. Pemberton sold the ownership rights to Asa Griggs Candler, a businessman, in 1888. Candler's marketing tactics led Coca-Cola to its dominance in the global soft-drink market throughout the 20th and 21st centuries.

The name refers to two of its original ingredients: coca leaves and kola nuts, a source of caffeine. The current formula of Coca-Cola remains a trade secret. A variety of reported recipes and experimental recreations have been published. The secrecy around the formula has been used by Coca-Cola in its marketing as only a handful of anonymous employees know the formula. The drink has inspired imitators and created the cola classification of soft drinks.

The company originally sold Coca-Cola syrup to independent bottling companies. Chattanooga was the site of the first Coca-Cola bottling company in 1889. The bottling companies eventually contracted with other suppliers. This contract specified that bottles would be sold at 5¢ each, without a fixed duration. This led to the fixed price of Coca-Cola from 1886 to 1959. The Coca-Cola Company merged with two of their largest bottling operators in 1986 to form Coca-Cola Enterprises Inc. (CCE).

The Coca-Cola Company was purchased in 1919 by a group of investors led by Ernest Woodruff's Trust Company for $25 million and reincorporated in Delaware. The company publicly offered 500,000 shares of the company for $40 a share. Robert W. Woodruff, Ernest's son, was elected President of the company in 1923. Woodruff expanded the company and brought Coca-Cola to the rest of the world. Coca-Cola began distributing bottles as "Six-packs," encouraging customers to purchase the beverage for their home.

Broader Context

It would be reasonable to claim that the New South also includes cities like Austin, Charlotte, Dallas, Houston, Orlando, Phoenix, and San Antonio. They are similar to Atlanta in terms of academic and business cultures, although their diversified economies differ substantially:

- Austin – technology, semiconductors
- Charlotte – banking, automotive, energy
- Dallas – technology, financial services and defense
- Houston – energy, aerospace
- Orlando – aerospace, defense
- Phoenix – electronics, mining, aerospace
- San Antonio – technology, aerospace

Unlike the Northeast, these metro areas do not cross state boundaries. Despite having highly ranked private universities such as Duke, Emory, Rice, and Vanderbilt, public institutions dominate higher education. Entrepreneurship is encouraged, but is not yet at the scale of Boston, New York, California, and Seattle. Compared to the Northeast, religious denominations play major social and cultural roles.

These cities are much newer than the Northeast cities, with extensive suburbs – and much traffic. Housing is much more affordable than in the Northeast. Pervasive strip malls in the suburbs tend to include the same stores across these cities. Consequently, the "look and feel" of these cities is rather homogenous.

All but Austin host professional sports teams. However, college sports overshadow these teams. The Southeastern Conference (SEC) has dominated the national collegiate football championship, with rare losses to teams from the Atlantic Coast Conference and Big Ten Conference. It has been argued that the SEC serves as the farm team for the National Football League.

Higher Education

Emory University was founded in 1836 in Oxford, Georgia, as Emory College by the Methodist Episcopal Church and named in honor of Methodist bishop John Emory. Emory moved to Atlanta in 1919 and is located in Druid Hills.

- Emory's School of Medicine opened its doors in 1915. The School of Medicine was initially located in a building formerly used by the Atlanta College of Medicine, which was located across the street from the relatively new Grady Memorial Hospital.
- The Emory Lamar School of Law was founded in 1916. The building provided for the law school was one of the original buildings on the Emory Quad – one that is now the Carlos Museum.
- The Emory School of Business Administration, known as Goizueta Business School since 1994, was founded in 1919 after the dean of Emory College recommended the Board of Trustees create a "school of economics and business administration."
- The Rollins School of Public Health at Emory was founded in 1990. The school has more than 1,100 students pursuing master's degrees and over 150 students pursuing doctorate degrees.

The Centers for Disease Control and Prevention (CDC) is adjacent to the Emory campus on Clifton Road. It is the national public health agency under the Department of Health and Human Services. Founded in 1946, the agency's mission is the protection of public health and safety through the control and prevention of disease, injury, and disability. It has roughly 11,000 employees and a budget of $11 billion. Several senior executives from CDC have become senior faculty members in Emory's schools of medicine and public health.

Georgia Institute of Technology was established in 1885 in Atlanta. It was named Georgia School of Technology until 1948. The new name was chosen to reflect a growing focus on advanced technological and scientific research. Women students were admitted in 1952, and in 1961 Georgia Tech became the first university in the Deep South to admit African-American students without a court order.

In contrast, Charlayne Hunter-Gault, who became a well-known journalist, was one of two black students who enrolled at the University of Georgia in 1961 following a court order. They had been denied admission. This led to the court case *Holmes v. Danner*, in which the registrar of the university, Walter Danner, was the defendant. After winning the case, Holmes and Hunter became the first two African-American students to enroll at the University of Georgia.

Georgia Tech's programs are dominated by engineering, science, and technology. Tech's top-ranked programs include the following, with founding dates indicated.

- School of Mechanical Engineering, 1888
- School of Civil & Environmental Engineering, 1896
- School of Electrical & Computer Engineering, 1896
- School of Chemical & Biomolecular Engineering, 1901
- School of Aerospace Engineering, 1930
- School of Industrial & Systems Engineering, 1945
- School of Material Science & Engineering, 1985
- School of Biomedical Engineering, 1997
- College of Computing, 1988

The School of Biomedical Engineering is a joint venture between Emory and Georgia Tech. The two universities share courses, faculty, and students. This makes particular sense as Emory does not have a School of Engineering and Georgia Tech does not have a School of Medicine.

The Georgia Tech Research Institute employs 2,800 researchers and staff with annual revenue exceeding $0.5 billion. They have pioneered the development and deployment of technologies for:

- Air pollution
- Antennas
- Drones
- Energy
- Poultry industry
- Prosthetics
- Radar enhancement
- Satellites
- Vehicle Design
- Wireless communications

The Atlanta University Center, located in the heart of the city, is the world's largest consortia of African American private institutions of higher education. Originally formed in 1929, the Consortium is a nonprofit organization that operates on behalf of its member institutions: Clark Atlanta University, Morehouse College, Morehouse School of Medicine, and Spelman College.

Atlanta University, founded in 1865, and Clark College, founded in 1869, merged to form Clark Atlanta University in 1988, a leading private, historically black doctoral research university. Morehouse College, established in 1867, is the nation's largest private liberal arts college for men. Formed in 1881, Spelman College is a highly selective liberal arts college for women.

The Consortium's newest member institution, Morehouse School of Medicine, was formed in 1974 and is one of the nation's most widely recognized community-based medical schools.

Sports

College football is the most popular sport in much of the South. Georgia Tech of the Atlantic Coast Conference has won the national championship four times. The University of Georgia of the SEC has won the national championship three times. The two schools are bitter rivals.

The Atlanta Braves baseball team of the National League has won the World Series twice. Atlanta United of Major League Soccer has won the championship once. The Atlanta Falcons have been to the Super Bowl twice, losing both times. The Atlanta Hawks have not won an NBA championship since moving to Atlanta from St. Louis.

Atlantans and southerners in general are rapid sports fans. Sports pubs with pervasive large screen televisions are packed for games. Tailgating in crowded parking lots outside stadia is a pregame specialty. Cooking grills provide the usual sporting fare and occasional gourmet offerings.

City Politics

Atlanta and Savannah are firmly Democrat. The suburbs were largely Republican but are moving toward Democrat. Rural Georgia is firmly Republican. Consequently, Georgia is a "purple" state. Democrat Joe Biden carried Georgia in 2020. The state's two US Senators are Democrats.

Historically, the southern states were controlled by conservative Democrats, often called Dixiecrats. That changed with Richard Nixon's southern strategy. It was the brainchild of Kevin Phillips. His 1969 book, *The Emerging Republican Majority*, provided the blueprint for the Republican Party to win over white voters who were alienated by the Democratic Party's embrace of civil rights in the 1960s.

Phillips advised Republicans to exploit the racial anxieties of white voters, linking them directly to issues such as crime, federal spending, and voting rights. The strategy, beginning with Nixon's landslide victory in the 1972 presidential race, helped produce GOP majorities for decades. The former Dixiecrat party is now the Republican Party in the South.

Abolitionist Era

When the settlement of Georgia was first envisioned in the early 1730s, slavery was banned in order to avoid the slave-based plantation economy that had developed in other colonies in the South. Unfortunately, the allure of profits from slavery proved too powerful for white Georgians to resist. By the era of the American Revolution (1775–1783), slavery was legal, and enslaved Africans constituted nearly half of Georgia's population.

While the Revolution fostered the growth of an antislavery movement in the northern states, white Georgia landowners fiercely maintained their commitment to slavery even as the war disrupted the plantation economy. Georgia delegates forced Thomas Jefferson to tone down the critique of slavery in his initial draft of the Declaration of Independence in 1776. At the subsequent constitutional convention in 1787, Georgia and South Carolina delegates inserted clauses protecting slavery in the new US Constitution.

Progressive Era

Most state governments, including Georgia's, generated Progressive reforms that often coincided with, but sometimes differed from, those enacted at the federal level. Major areas of economic, social, and moral reform among southern states included prohibition, woman suffrage, the regulation of child labor, campaigns to abolish the convict lease system and reform of the penal system, and expansion of educational opportunities and social services for marginalized groups.

Progressive urban reformers in cities like Atlanta and Augusta turned to the principles of business efficiency as a good guide for government. They improved sewer lines and streets, added parks, and undertook city beautification projects. The goal was to create more livable cities, though not for all. There was little discussion, at first, of working conditions, hours, or wages for mill, factory, and lumber workers or for domestic servants and the poor.

Paradoxically, the disfranchisement of black voters was considered a reform by white progressives in southern states who felt that it eliminated a major source of electoral corruption. Segregation laws imposed at the same time were also viewed as progressive by those who saw them as the only means by which racial peace could be achieved. It is rather difficult to believe that this line of reasoning was broadly accepted.

Progressives included not only political leaders – governors, legislators, and mayors – but also academics, educators, businessmen, large farmers, and both women and black activists. All of these groups shared a basic belief in "energetic government"; they recognized both the responsibility and the ability of government, at federal, state, and local levels, to solve the many social, economic, and political problems that faced the rapidly modernizing nation at the turn of the century.

Civil Rights Era

Civil rights were slow to be realized in Atlanta, despite the fact that Constitutional Amendment 13 (1865) abolished slavery, Amendment 14 (1868) provided citizenship to everyone born in the United States, and Amendment 15 (1870) gave black Americans the right to vote.

As an example of this slow pace, in 1948 African American citizens in Atlanta used their voting power to negotiate the hiring of eight African American policemen. By 1960 African American policemen increased to only 31, and black and white officers did not begin working together until 1969.

In 1960 the City of Atlanta had 42 parks for whites and only three for blacks, 12 swimming pools for whites and three for blacks, 16 recreation centers for whites and three for blacks. There were 4,000 hospital beds available for whites and only 780 available for blacks. Despite some 300,000 African American citizens of Atlanta, there were no African Americans serving on the Atlanta Board of Aldermen, Board of Education, nor the boards for Recreation, the Library, and Public Welfare.

A major proponent of continued segregation in the South was the local government's reluctance – and often outright refusal – to enforce its own laws. Even after the Supreme Court had ruled against segregated schools in 1954, Atlanta schools remained segregated until 1961. Likewise, Grady Hospital was ordered by the Supreme Court to desegregate all of its facilities in 1962; Grady did not desegregate in full until 1965.

Challenges

All ecosystems have economic, political, and environmental challenges, but the nature of these challenges tends to differ based on the characteristics of the ecosystem.

Economic Challenges

Metro Atlanta is known as an affordable place to live, but housing costs are rising, threatening to erode this competitive advantage. Housing is generally considered affordable if a family spends less than 30% of its income on rent or a mortgage and other housing costs. By that definition, most metro Atlanta neighborhoods are not affordable for families earning less than $50,000 a year. Income inequality exacerbates this challenge. Median household income for a white family exceeds $80,000, compared to less than $30,000 for a black family.

The Atlanta region is a leader in job growth, but too many good jobs are going unfilled. More than half of the advertised jobs in the region require at least a bachelor's degree, while only 35% of residents over age 25 meet that requirement. At the same time, many residents are not getting the skills needed to land a well-paying job. Matching available jobs and qualified workers is a significant challenge.

An expanded regional transit network is critical to keeping metro Atlanta economically competitive, which will require implementing transit funding and governance. This will involve accommodating increasing freight traffic. Because of its size and its position as a crossroads for highway, rail, air, and ocean-going goods, the Atlanta region is the Southeast's most important freight hub. That reputation will certainly need to be continued in the future and require sustained investments.

Online retailers have disrupted brick-and-mortar stores, and now they are changing city traffic patterns and land use as well. E-commerce has grown to such an extent, according to retail and logistics experts, that metro Atlanta and other big cities will have to grapple with vacant storefronts, new types of warehouses, and changing delivery routes. The rapid pace of change will challenge transportation and urban planners to keep up.

Preparing for autonomous and connected vehicles will be a challenge. Cutting-edge advancements in the future include self-driving vehicles, "smart" signals that optimize traffic flow, and connected cars that "talk" to each other and avoid collisions.

The Atlanta region is one of the fastest-growing in the nation, but the long-term economic success of a large segment of our population is uncertain because of the rise of automation in the workplace. Preparing for this future will be challenging.

Political Challenges

When asked about the biggest challenges facing metro Atlanta, 27% of the respondents said crime and public safety, 24% said the economy, and 11% said transportation, reflecting perennial frustration with traffic congestion.

Improving K-12 educational outcomes is an essential challenge. Increasing readiness for college and career is critical to the region's future. The Atlanta region must work to improve third-grade reading skills, which are key to long-term student success, and also take advantage of the state's expanding technical college system to better meet the needs of today's employers.

Metro Atlanta is experiencing an unprecedented demographic shift as Baby Boomers age and better health allows people to live longer than ever before. By 2030, one out of every five residents will be over the age of 60. The region needs to foster communities that work for all ages and abilities.

Environmental Challenges

The population of the 15-county region is forecasted to increase by nearly 3 million people by 2050. Securing a clean, abundant water supply is vital to the Atlanta region's economic future. This is critically important as metro Atlanta continues to grow.

Remediating sewage pollution in Atlanta is an ongoing, decades-long struggle. While some communities have seen major improvements in water quality, marginalized communities in west and south Atlanta are still burdened with disproportionate levels of sewage pollution.

Vehicular emissions are the leading cause of pollution in Atlanta, ranking 2nd nationally for most air pollution from motor vehicles. This emission source is often blamed for Atlanta's ozone challenges. Enhanced public transit and increasing use of electric vehicles are needed.

Weather disruptions to the transportation system negatively impact the quality of life and the economic viability of the Atlanta region. Flooding, snow and ice storms, and heat waves all disrupt travel and impact residents and travelers alike. The region needs to be better equipped to address disruptions. Currently, the city is completely ill-equipped to deal with snow and ice.

Innovation Outlook

I moved to Atlanta in 1981 to join the faculty at Georgia Tech. We moved our company Search Technology, Inc. from Illinois to Georgia at the same time. Sibling companies, Search Aeronautics, Inc. and Enterprise Support Systems, Inc., were formed in the 1990s, spinning off technologies developed in the parent company.

It was exciting to participate in the Atlanta technology community during these early years. Meet and greet events were frequent. Mentoring was readily available. Georgia Tech served as a vibrant hub. Available venture funding was modest, but angel investors were pervasive.

With strong connections to Georgia Tech, workforce development was straightforward. Engineering coops filled our ranks, many transitioning to full-time employees when they graduated. Mentoring young engineers and computer scientists was a significant role for our senior technical staff members.

Venture Capital Funding

Venture capital funding in states with historically strong startup ecosystems declined from 2021 to 2022, likely due economic impacts of the coronavirus pandemic. For 2023, Atlanta companies are on track to nearly hit $4 billion in capital raised. Information technology, business services, and health and life sciences account for roughly three-quarters of venture capital investments.

Growth Opportunities

Financial and tech firms continue to flock toward metro Atlanta. This builds on the city's strong logistics, entertainment and film, and health services industries. Demand for quality housing in the region has become fierce, particularly in the city center. Thus, projections for housing demands will remain strong.

I consider four growth opportunities for the innovation assessment in the next section. The first focuses on workforce development. There is a need for a multifaceted approach to grow the workforce by engaging workers of all kinds, including newcomers to the state and those who are currently out of the labor force, voluntarily or otherwise. This approach should be based on a deep understanding of how best to address engagement.

The second opportunity is healthcare. Investments are needed in healthcare infrastructure that enables and encourages the use of preventive care to offset the rising impact of noncommunicable diseases, as well as support the needs of disabled and older adults. The needed infrastructure will likely be substantially technology enabled. Additional economic value will be created in the process.

Education is the third opportunity. Building on the state's strength in higher education, the emphasis needs to broaden with a focus on part-time programs and adult learning opportunities. Efforts to address learning gaps in the K–12 system should be emphasized to create leading-edge capabilities both before college and during college or technical education.

Healthcare and education services can be greatly enhanced by leading-edge technologies that I describe in detail in Chapter 8. Indeed, Georgia Tech has been a strong contributor to many of these developments, which are applicable to all of the innovation ecosystems, but are better explained once rather than repeatedly.

The fourth opportunity is transportation. Using investments in airports, roads and bridges, and public transit, as well as rail, air, and sea-going capabilities, options should be developed and resources committed to help. It is essential to ensure that the state's transportation infrastructure remains nationally and internationally competitive and continues to pay off. This has long been a strong suit of Georgia in general, and Atlanta and Savannah in particular, and these competitive advantages need to be sustained.

Innovation Assessment

Table 6.1 summarizes an assessment of growth opportunities in workforce, healthcare, education, and transportation.

Workforce strengths include abundant employment opportunities, while weaknesses involve less than optimal workforce engagement. Education and training can remediate this disconnect, but the incumbent public K-12

Table 6.1   Innovation Assessment for New South

	Innovation Outlook			
	Workforce	*Healthcare*	*Education*	*Transportation*
Strengths	Employment Opportunities	Strong Health Centers	Higher Education	Excellent Installed Base
Weaknesses	Workforce Engagement	Much Too Labor Intensive	K-12 Education	Upgrades Needed
Opportunities	Education & Training	Preventive Care	Educational Technologies	More Transit Options
Threats	Current K-12 Education	System Fragmentation	System Fragmentation	Other Transit Hubs

education system has not been up to this challenge and may threaten this possibility by clinging to the status quo.

Healthcare can build on strong health centers in metro Atlanta. However, costs are very high due to the labor intensity of delivery processes, which will be exacerbated by an aging population. Increased emphasis on preventative care, likely technology enabled, can provide better care at lower costs. However, the fragmentation of much of the US delivery system may undermine this. The pervasive fee-for-service mentality in the US needs to be replaced by value-based care, whereby providers are paid for health outcomes.

Georgia is also blessed with an excellent installed base of transportation infrastructure. However, technology and market trends are creating pressure for substantial upgrades. For example, the vehicle-based pollution challenges noted earlier could be mitigated, in part, by more public transit options that would make the MARTA rail and bus system much more pervasive, perhaps modeled on the Washington, DC Metro system. Other transit hubs are investing, in part, due to the federal infrastructure bill, and Georgia needs to keep up with competitors' initiatives.

The greatest risk for metro Atlanta is that the rich list of challenges will dilute investments in priority growth opportunities. At one level, this might result in peanut buttering financial resources across too many initiatives. More importantly, however, this might undermine growth opportunities by diluting the leadership, management, and technical talents needed by the priority opportunities. Money matters, but talent gets things done.

We see this phenomenon pervasively in the US Congress. Wars, as well as health, economic, and environmental crises, seem to enable focus and top talent to be aligned with the targeted foci. However, once such demands seem to pass, the agenda of less than high priority topics reappears and the dilution of human and financial resources is once again rampant. It takes strong leadership and discipline to avoid this. Such leadership and discipline are needed at local, state, and federal levels, across parties, advocacy groups, and other stakeholders.

Epilogue

The New South has much to build upon, including an increasingly competitive technology community and a strong – and affordable – system of higher education. Yet there are some lingering southern tendencies that would be better left behind. Of course, this is easier said than done.

I have found that appearance, conformity, and winning are very strong values in the New South. Women especially, but also men, tend to be fashionable and well groomed. Conformity on political, social, and religious beliefs tends to be expected, not enforced but expected.

People tend to be very polite, but you do not know what they are really thinking. Thus, you may think you have reached an agreement but have not. This contrasts with Gotham where people tell you exactly what they think, whether you like it or not. More on this later.

Winning is very important, personally, in business and sports. They let you know, often rather indirectly, where they and their children went to college, the success of their business ventures, and the notable wins of their sports teams, particularly college sports. Unlike Gotham, they do not explicitly share their net worth.

The fact that many people are not winning, that many people in metro Atlanta struggle with poor health, education, and jobs, is attributed to a lack of gumption. After all, they pulled themselves up by their bootstraps, despite their parents having graduated from Harvard and having substantial incomes.

When I moved to Atlanta in the early 1980s, I was surprised to encounter the Ku Klux Klan in their full regalia soliciting donations at traffic lights south of the city. I had thought those days were long gone. However, it seems the Republican's southern strategy may have encouraged it.

Outside of metro Atlanta, as well as central Savannah, the Old South is still a significant force. Indeed, reverence for the former Confederacy is pervasive across the rural South. White Supremacy often is influential. Republicans have known since Nixon that appeals to these tendencies will garner many votes.

Chapter 7

Gotham

"Gotham" is a nickname for New York City that first became popular when writer Washington Irving attached it to New York in 1807. Irving took the name from the village of Gotham, Nottinghamshire in England: a place inhabited, according to folklore, by fools. Gotham City is the home of Batman. It is claimed to be in New Jersey, but is visually depicted as Manhattan.

The New York metropolitan area is the city and suburbs of New York City, and Long Island and the Mid- and Lower Hudson Valley in the state of New York. It also includes north and central New Jersey, three counties in western Connecticut, and five counties in northeastern Pennsylvania. About 24 million people populate metropolitan New York.

I lived in Hoboken, NJ, for five years. It is effectively a sixth borough of New York City. Every weekday morning a large proportion of Hoboken's 60,000 residents drain from the city, via subways and ferries, to commute to their jobs in Manhattan. The view east from Hoboken is a dramatic panorama of Manhattan, particularly vivid at night.

Early Settlement

The first humans arrived in the region as early as 9,000 years ago, but the area was abandoned, likely due to the extinction of many large game species that were a source of food. A second wave of inhabitants arrived approximately 3,000 years ago and left behind the remains of many early

DOI: 10.4324/9781003507468-7

encampments. The region has probably remained continually inhabited from that time.

By the time of the arrival of Europeans, the Lenape were cultivating fields of vegetation through the slash-and-burn technique. This extended the productive life of planted fields. They also harvested vast quantities of fish and shellfish from the bays of the area. These methods allowed the inhabitants to maintain a larger population than nomadic hunter-gatherers elsewhere could support.

It has been estimated that at the time of European settlement, there may have been about 15,000 Lenape tribe members in numerous settlement sites around much of New York City. In 1524 Lenape in canoes met Giovanni da Verrazzano, the first European explorer to enter New York Harbor.

In 1613, the Dutch established a trading post on the western shore of Manhattan Island. The New Netherland company was established in 1614. It was not until 1623 that the Dutch interests in the area were other than commercial. Fort Amsterdam was built in 1624. Within a year, a small settlement, called New Amsterdam, had grown around the fort. In 1626, Peter Minuit purchased Manhattan Island and Staten Island from native people in exchange for trade goods.

The British captured the city in 1664 and renamed it New York. The British evacuated the city in 1783, nearly three months after the Treaty of Paris was signed ending the American Revolutionary War. New York ratified the U.S. Constitution in 1788, becoming the 11th of the original 13 states to join the Union.

Cities and Towns

Manhattan is the cultural, administrative, and financial center of New York City and hosts the headquarters of many major multinational corporations, the United Nations Headquarters, Wall Street, and a number of well-known universities. Manhattan is often considered by some to be the cultural, financial, media, and entertainment capital of the world.

The Bronx is the only New York City borough that is part of the US mainland. It is the location of Yankee Stadium, home of the New York Yankees. It is also home to the Bronx Zoo, the world's largest metropolitan zoo. Directly to the zoo's north is the New York Botanical Garden, a

National Historic Landmark. Pelham Bay Park is the largest park in New York City.

Brooklyn is known for its cultural, social, and ethnic diversity, an independent art scene, distinct neighborhoods, and distinctive architectural heritage. Downtown Brooklyn is the largest neighborhood in the outer boroughs. The borough has a long beachfront shoreline including Coney Island, established in the 1870s as one of the earliest amusement parks in the country.

Queens is geographically the largest borough, the most ethnically diverse county in the United States, as well as the most ethnically diverse urban area in the world. Historically a collection of small towns and villages founded by the Dutch, the borough has since developed both commercial and residential prominence.

Staten Island is the most suburban in character of the five boroughs. Staten Island is connected to Brooklyn by the Verrazzano-Narrows Bridge and to Manhattan by way of the Staten Island Ferry, a free commuter ferry. This popular tourist attraction provides unobstructed views of the Statue of Liberty, Ellis Island, and Lower Manhattan. The Staten Island Greenbelt includes 28 miles of walking trails and one of the last undisturbed forests in the city.

As mentioned earlier, the city Hoboken and neighboring Jersey City represent a sixth borough in that their residents relate – practically and perhaps emotionally – to Manhattan, rather than New Jersey, for employment, shopping, and entertainment. Unlike the rest of the state, people can easily avoid the cost and stress of car ownership. Public transportation is excellent.

Economic Base

The economy of New York City encompasses the largest municipal and regional economy in the United States. In 2022, its GDP was $2.1 trillion. Anchored by Wall Street in Lower Manhattan, New York City has been characterized as the world's premier financial center. The New York Stock Exchange (NYSE) and Nasdaq, the world's two largest stock exchanges by both market capitalization and trading activity, are based in the city.

J.P. MORGAN & COMPANY

Junius S. Morgan joined George Peabody & Co. in 1854 to form Peabody, Morgan & Co. Junius took control of the firm in 1864 on Peabody's retirement, changing its name to J.S. Morgan & Co. Junius's son, J. Pierpont Morgan, founded his own firm, J. Pierpont Morgan & Company, in 1864. J. Pierpont Morgan & Company traded in government bonds and foreign exchange. On Junius's death in 1890, Pierpont Morgan took his place and reorganized in 1895 as J.P. Morgan and Company.

In 1892, the company began to finance the New York, New Haven, and Hartford Railroad and made it the dominant railroad in New England. General Electric was formed through the 1892 merger of Edison General Electric Company and Thomson-Houston Electric Company, with Charles Coffin, Edison, and J.P. Morgan as cofounders.

In 1895, during the depression that followed the panic of 1893, the firm supplied the United States government with $62 million in gold to float a bond issue and restore the treasury surplus of $100 million. It also organized the financial community to avert a financial collapse after the market panic of 1907.

The firm financed the formation of the United States Steel Corporation in 1901, combining the business of Andrew Carnegie and others to create the world's first billion-dollar corporation. In 1902, J.P. Morgan merged the McCormick Harvesting Machine Company and Deering Harvester Company, along with three smaller agricultural equipment firms, to form International Harvester.

In 1933, provisions of the Glass–Steagall Act forced J.P. Morgan & Co. to separate its investment banking from its commercial banking operations. J.P. Morgan & Co. chose to operate as a commercial bank. The firm made the decision to spin off its investment banking operations to form Morgan Stanley. In 2000, Chase Manhattan Bank, looking to improve its position in investment banking, merged with J.P. Morgan to form JPMorgan Chase & Co.

New York City is the world's leading center of banking, finance, and communications. Many of the world's largest corporations are headquartered in Manhattan. The city is distinctive for its high concentrations of advanced service sector firms in law, accountancy, banking, and management consultants. It is the top global center for the advertising industry, often called Madison Avenue. Silicon Alley is used to characterize the city's expanding broad-spectrum high technology sphere.

Finance, health care and life sciences, high technology and biotechnology, real estate, and insurance, all are central to New York City's economy. The city is also the nation's most important center for mass media, journalism, and publishing, as well as the country's preeminent arts center. Creative industries such as digital media, advertising, fashion, design, and architecture account for a growing share of employment, with strong competitive advantages in these industries.

The Port of New York and New Jersey is a major economic engine, handling a maritime cargo volume in 2022 of roughly 10 million twenty-foot equivalent units (TEUs), a critical metric in the container shipping industry. The port has benefitted from the expansion of the Panama Canal, accelerating ahead of California seaports in monthly cargo volumes.

Innovation Heritage

When I first moved to the area in 2012, I was soon invited to provide a lecture on "How Greater New York City Transformed America" at the New York Yacht Club. I decided to focus on 34 innovators over 200 years in nine different market domains. I delivered this lecture in the Model Room of the New York Yacht Club, which houses 1,340 scaled yacht replicas, of which 150 are full-hulled and rigged models, with the balance half-models. Several of the models on the walls belonged to the luminaries discussed below.

I was subsequently invited to give this talk several times. One of the most memorable times was at the Chart House in Weehawken on the Hudson River. My dinner talk to a group of insurance executives was highlighted by the New York City skyline behind me and ablaze with neon. It made the overall story rather dramatic.

Ships and Railroads

I started this story with John Stevens (1749–1838) who innovated in shipping and railroads. Peter Cooper (1791–1883) introduced the first US steam locomotive and founded Cooper Union in 1853. Cornelius Vanderbilt (1794–1877) was the first tycoon in shipping and railroads. Shipbuilding moved to Maine, Louisiana, Philadelphia, and Virginia, although the Port of New York and New Jersey is stronger than ever in terms of container shipping. Railroads moved everywhere – that, of course, is their purpose.

Clothes and Personal Care

John Jacob Astor (1763–1848) was America's first millionaire, made in the fur industry. C.J. Walker (1867–1919) was the first African American woman millionaire, an innovator in beauty products. Hattie Carnegie (1880–1956) pioneered ready-to-wear clothes; she designed the Woman's Army Corps uniform. Charles Revson (1906–1975) founded Revlon Cosmetics. New York City is still a major player in fashion, clothes, and cosmetics, epitomized by the bi-annual New York Fashion Week, which provides leading designers from around the world with an unrivaled global platform to showcase their collections.

Pharmaceuticals

Charles Pfizer (1824–1906) founded Pfizer. Robert Wood Johnson (1845–1910) founded Johnson & Johnson. George W. Merck (1894–1957) founded Merck. New York City, along with New Jersey, remains a major player in the pharmaceutical industry.

Buildings and Builders

John Roebling (1806–1869) designed the Brooklyn Bridge. Elisha Otis (1811–1861) invented elevators. Willis Carrier (1876–1950) invented modern air conditioning. William Lamb (1883–1952) was the architect of the Empire State Building and other skyscrapers. Robert Moses (1888–1981) was known as the master builder. He brought two Worlds Fairs and the United Nations Headquarters to New York City. The city is inherently a major player in this domain, with new major buildings constantly being erected.

Oil and Refining

John D. Rockefeller (1839–1913) was the first tycoon of the oil industry, forming Standard Oil Trust, which monopolized the industry. The Supreme Court found Standard Oil in violation of the Sherman Antitrust Act in 1911 and split the enterprise into 34 independent companies. Standard Oil of New Jersey became Esso, which is now ExxonMobil. Carleton Ellis (1876–1941) founded Ellis Laboratories in New Jersey and invented the continuous thermal cracking process central to oil refining. Oil and refining moved to Oklahoma, Texas, and the Gulf Coast in general to be closer to energy sources. Houston is now seen as a leading energy city.

Electricity, Computers, and Communications

Thomas Edison (1847–1931), wizard of Menlo Park, created the electric lighting industry. Nicola Tesla (1856–1943) innovated in electricity, wireless communications, and radio. Thomas J. Watson (1874–1956), called the world's greatest salesman, led the growth of IBM. Bell Labs (1925–1984), the idea factory, pioneered in the telephone and electronics industry.

Computing expanded to California (Apple) and Washington State (Microsoft) in particular. Communications services remain a strong element of the New York economy. IBM is still headquartered in Armonk, New York, but focuses more on technical services than hardware and software.

Finance and Banking

J. Pierpont Morgan (1837–1913) was the first tycoon of the finance industry, lending money to the federal government during the crises of 1895 and 1907. Alfred Winslow Jones (1900–1989) was the father of the hedge fund industry. Walter Wriston (1919–2005) was CEO of Citicorp who introduced ATMs, CDs, credit cards, and interstate banking. Fisher Black, Myron Scholes, and Robert Merton pioneered finance and options pricing models. Michael Bloomberg innovated in financial data services. New York City remains a dominant global player in the industry.

Academics and Activists

Theodore Roosevelt (1838–1919), 26th US President, was the first American to win a Nobel Prize (Peace). Eleanor Roosevelt (1884–1962) was first lady (1933–1945) and an author and civil rights activist. Margaret Mead (1901–1978) was an academic anthropologist who broadened views. Rosalyn Yalow (1921–2011) was an innovator and won a Nobel Prize in medicine.

The list of innovators in this arena could be very long and New York City is inherently a major player. The issues and personalities, of course, change. However, the city can always be counted on to have opinions and be willing to express them. Journalism outlets such as the *New York Times* and *Wall Street Journal* are among many venues for such content.

Aviation

Leroy Grumman (1895–1982) founded Grumman Aeronautical Engineering. Frederick B. Rentschler (1887–1956) founded Pratt & Whitney Aircraft. Igor Sikorsky (1889–1972) invented helicopters. Juan Trippe (1889–1981) founded Pan American World Airways. Aviation moved west, primarily to California and Washington State where a wealth of aerospace firms were founded.

Broader Context

The top 25 companies in NYC have over $1 trillion in annual revenues. Banking and finance, insurance, and communications account for 73%. Pharmaceuticals, investments, entertainment, and consumer products account for 27%.

Aviation, computers, electronics, energy, railroads, and shipbuilding are legacies that greater New York City provided America. New York City seems to have been particularly good at incubating innovations.

Metro Gotham includes New York City, of course, but, as noted earlier, also western Connecticut, northern New Jersey, and northern Pennsylvania. Some argue for the inclusion of southern New Jersey and Pennsylvania, bringing Philadelphia into the ecosystem.

The metro region includes over 24 million people, with a GDP of over $2 trillion. The "Acela Corridor" from Boston to Washington includes 50 million people, with a GDP of $6 trillion, roughly 25% of the national GDP but only 2% of the US land area. Thus, the region disproportionately contributes to the nation's economic health.

Gotham clearly is a very rich business ecosystem. It generates 56% of California's GDP on 8% of its land area. Yet, like California, it suffers from very high costs of living and taxation, especially property taxes. Unlike California, metro New York has a robust public transportation system, albeit often very crowded.

Bodies of Water

The island of Manhattan is bordered by the Hudson River on the west, the East River on the southeast, and the Harlem River on the east and northeast. The perimeter of Manhattan is 32 miles. Staten Island and New Jersey are to the west of the Hudson, Brooklyn and Queens to the south of the East River, and the Bronx to the east of the Harlem River.

The East River connects to Long Island Sound, which connects to the Atlantic Ocean. The East River is heavily traveled with commercial traffic, primarily tugs with tows, hi-speed ferries, and a few deep draft ships. It was used to provide the passageway for steamships back and forth between New York and Boston.

One of the bodies of water most significant to New York City was the Erie Canal, a historic canal in upstate New York that runs east–west between the Hudson River at Albany and Lake Erie. Completed in 1825, the canal was the first navigable waterway connecting the Atlantic Ocean to the Great Lakes, vastly reducing the costs of transporting people and goods across the Appalachians.

The cargo transported on the Erie Canal vaulted New York City ahead of Boston, Philadelphia, and Charleston to become the top port on the east coast, a distinction New York retains, with one footnote. When container ships became the norm, Manhattan did not have enough space to accommodate them. Consequently, New York and New Jersey formed a combined Port Authority that has thrived.

Crossing Bodies of Water

Traveling in greater New York City often requires crossing bodies of water. Bridges, tunnels, and ferries enable this. The island of Manhattan is connected to the rest of the city through 21 bridges and 15 tunnels. Traffic backups are often problematic.

George Washington Bridge crosses the Hudson from New Jersey to Manhattan. As noted earlier, the Verrazzano-Narrows Bridge connects the New York City boroughs of Staten Island and Brooklyn. The Brooklyn Bridge and the Williamsburg Bridge span the East River between the boroughs of Manhattan and Brooklyn. The Bronx–Whitestone Bridge connects the Bronx to Queens.

Train tunnels under the Hudson include Amtrak and the PATH Subway. There are four tunnels under the East River for trains to and from the east. Several subway trains cross the river on bridges. The Holland and Lincoln tunnels serve automobiles between New Jersey and Manhattan. The Queens Midtown Tunnel runs under the East River.

There are numerous ferries including the famous Staten Island Ferry. New York Waterway has several routes between New Jersey and Manhattan. East River ferries connect to several locations in Brooklyn and Queens.

Higher Education

There are over 200 colleges and universities in metropolitan New York City. Three of the eight Ivy League institutions are within the metro area, broadly defined. Columbia is in uptown Manhattan. Yale is on the eastern fringe of the region. Princeton is on the southern fringe.

With more than 65,000 students attending its nearly 20 schools and colleges, New York University (NYU) is among the largest private schools in the United States. City College (CCNY) is a public research university within the City University of New York system. City College was the first free public institution of higher education in the United States.

The average annual cost at NYU, after aid, is $40,000, while the average annual cost at CCNY is $2,000. The Cooper Union for the Advancement of Science and Art (CU) was mentioned earlier. With Peter Cooper's endowment, along with subsequent gifts, the school was able to fund a full-tuition scholarship for each of its undergraduate students. Beginning in 2014, CU now offers a half-tuition scholarship to each admitted student. The average annual cost at CU, after aid, is $11,000.

Gotham Politics

Five US presidents were born in New York:

- Martin Van Buren – 8th US President (1837–1841). Born in Kinderhook in 1782.
- Millard Fillmore – 13th US President (1850–1853). Born in Summer Hill in 1800.
- Theodore Roosevelt – 26th US President (1901–1909). Born in New York City in 1858.
- Franklin Roosevelt – 32nd US President (1933–1945). Born in Hyde Park in 1882.
- Donald Trump – 45th US President (2017–2021). Born in Queens in 1946.

State Politics

New York state politics has generally been defined by strong Democratic Party control in New York City and dominance by the Republican Party upstate and on Long Island. Since 1920 both Democratic and Republican governors have held power and the legislature has tended to be Republican-dominated, although since the mid-1970s the Assembly has tended to be controlled by the Democrats. Both the Democrats and the Republicans have strong statewide party organizations.

City Politics

The history of the government of New York City is also the history of the misgovernment of New York City. The story of municipal corruption is the story of the bosses who have organized and profited from that corruption. It is the story of the contractors who have gotten rich from their arrangements with the bosses. The people of New York City shrugged their shoulders and went about their business.

The Society of Saint Tammany was organized in New York City in May of 1789. Tammany was a legendary chief of the Delaware Indians whose benevolence and love of liberty led to the establishment of patriotic societies during that period. The best known of Tammany's early leaders was Aaron Burr. Tammany was a tool of the state machine, which Martin Van Buren had organized in the decade before his election to the Senate. As noted above, he was later elected President of the United States.

Tammany took command in 1851 with the election of a City Council that soon won the nickname of the Forty Thieves. Padded bills, bribery, and kickbacks from contractors were routine. In 1857, the Republican-dominated state legislature passed a series of laws that set the stage for the rise of the most notorious band of rascals in the city's history. A Board of Supervisors was established – a board that served as the main link between the city and the state. It was led by a Democrat, the rising young Tammany politician named William Marcy Tweed.

After two years of service on the New York City Council, Tweed was elected to Congress in 1852. Washington seems not to have offered the kind of opportunities that he expected from a political career, and he returned to New York. There he obtained an appointment as a commissioner on the Board of Education. In addition, in 1857 he became a member of the newly formed Board of Supervisors.

One function of the board was to audit bills presented to the city for payment. Soon Tweed had organized a "ring" of supervisors who voted together on these bills. Contractors who wanted to do business with the city found themselves obliged to pad their invoices and, when the city paid, to kick back a part of the padding to the ring. Tweed later apologized for the simplicity of the scheme: "It was just for making money," he said, "not for controlling politics."

By the end of 1863, Tweed had become both the grand sachem of Tammany and the chairman of the central committee of the New York County Democratic Party. That unusual double honor left little doubt who ruled as the "boss" in New York City politics. Over the next few years, the Supervisors' Ring gave way to the more formidable and more famous Tweed Ring, which existed both to make money and to control politics.

The elections of 1868 gave the Democratic Party a majority in both houses of the New York State Legislature. Tweed was in the state senate, and in 1870 he steered through the legislature a new charter for his city. The charter returned to New York much of the power that the charter of 1857 had taken away, and it placed the entire control of the city's finances in the hands of a new Board of Apportionment consisting of the mayor, the comptroller, the commissioner of the Parks Department, and the commissioner of the Department of Public Works. Tweed reportedly paid approximately one million dollars in bribes to get the new charter.

During the approximately 80 years between the founding of modern Tammany in the early 1850s and the inauguration of Fiorello H. La Guardia as mayor in 1934, anti-Tammany reformers held power for only ten years. Tammany's power was based on giving people what they wanted. For the immigrants who poured into New York in the last decades of the 19th century, what was wanted was the help of the most basic kind – finding a first job or a first place to live, finding food, and filling out citizenship papers. Tammany delivered. All it asked in exchange was a vote.

This chronicle provides the flavor of New York City politics. The issues and characters change, and such blatant corruption seems to have been mitigated. However, as with the story of Chicago politics in Chapter 4, power and control of enormous public resources seems to precipitate a tendency to deploy them for political and personal ends.

Abolitionist Era

Slavery was present in New York City from its earliest European settlement, with the first enslaved people brought to New Amsterdam in 1626. Total emancipation was not achieved until 1827. In 1835, abolitionists established the New York Committee of Vigilance, which later became part of the Underground Railroad. The group protected escaped slaves from slave catchers and often facilitated their subsequent journeys to upstate New York or New England.

Progressive Era

New York, in the late Gilded Age and Progressive Era, was the nation's principal hub for immigration. It was a center of civic engagement, where most of the nation's main reform organizations were headquartered. The city championed the fight for civil rights through the National Association for the Advancement of Colored People and the National Urban League. They sought solutions to labor problems through the American Association for Labor Legislation, the National Consumers' League, and the National Child Labor Committee. The city founded the nation's first settlement houses and established the first center for social science and social work.

Civil Rights Era

The first civil rights laws since Reconstruction were passed in New York City and the state, including the first fair housing, employment, and education laws. These inspired similar laws in dozens of other states and became models for national legislation in the 1960s. Nevertheless, tension and conflicts remain to this day and underlie continuing national frustrations.

Wealthier blacks moved into Harlem, due to the great migration of the early and mid-20th century, causing a tremendous increase in the black population of the city. Black churches played a key role in creating black Harlem since they bought the property at depreciated prices and helped many blacks settle there.

The New York Race Riots of 1964 were the first in a series of devastating race-related riots that ripped through American cities between 1964 and 1965. The riots began in Harlem, New York, following the shooting of 15-year-old James Powell by a white off-duty police officer in July of 1964. Significant national legislation soon followed in 1965, and 1968.

Challenges

All ecosystems have economic, political, and environmental challenges, but the nature of these challenges tends to differ based on the characteristics of the ecosystem.

Economic Challenges

Immigration poses major economic challenges for New York City. The city's population is 36% foreign born, gaining roughly 100,000 people per year. Migrants appear to choose New York City due to the city's "right to shelter" mandate, a court-ordered obligation to find placement for asylum seekers.

There are roughly 200,000 subsidized public housing units out of a total of 500,000 affordable units. There is an overall shortage of rental housing, with prices reflecting the city's very high cost of living. These costs, when combined with very high city and state taxes, make it difficult for many people to afford to live in the city.

The city is heavily dependent on public transportation. The New York City Subway is one of the world's oldest public transit systems, one of the most used, and the one with the most stations, with 472 stations in operation. It includes $1 trillion of underground assets. The system is congested and dirty, as well as reliant on outdated control systems, and needs major upgrades.

Political Challenges

The economic challenges are major contributors to the city's fiscal difficulties. Housing challenges lead to crowding. Traffic congestion in Manhattan can be intense, but mechanisms to decrease private vehicles in the city are politically unpopular. Pollution and air quality suffer from there being so many fossil-fueled vehicles. Public education is very uneven in quality and access. Crime is a perennial challenge.

Environmental Challenges

Environmental events, for example, Hurricane Sandy in 2012, can be enormously damaging. Underground assets such as the subways and tunnels are very difficult to fully protect. The average elevation of the southern part of Manhattan is 3–6 ft. Sea level rise due to melting Arctic and Antarctic ice caps will eventually exceed these levels. Protecting the city will be a major economic, political, and environmental challenge.

Innovation Outlook

Venture Capital Funding

With $104 billion, California leads in venture investments. New York is second with $29 billion. Massachusetts is third with $21 billion, while Illinois is fourth with $10 billion. Our other innovation ecosystems include North Carolina (tenth for $4.4 billion), Georgia (fifteenth for $2.3 billion), and Washington, DC (twenty-first for $1.4 billion). Of course, one can argue that some ecosystems, particularly Washington, DC, have significant other sources of investments.

Growth Opportunities

Banking and finance represents the city's dominant strong suit. With several of the world's top hospitals and academic health centers, New York City is well positioned in health care and life sciences, as well as high technology and biotechnology. However, there are many strong competitors across the United States, particularly in the Shining City.

Real estate has been a strong suit, but sky-high rents and post-pandemic occupancy challenges are significant risks. Insurance has also been a strong suit, but the city does not dominate as it does in banking and finance. We have found, for example, that insurance revenue will be decimated once driverless cars effectively eliminate accidents.

The city's strong positions in mass media, journalism, and publishing can provide a strong base for growth. However, this arena is being strongly driven by technology. Online platforms have long been displacing print. Streaming is decimating broadcast networks. Gamification is transforming the film industry. New York City has great track records in these domains, but there are many talented competitors.

Innovation Assessment

Table 7.1 summarizes an assessment of the innovation potential for banking and finance, insurance, and media and publishing. Banking and finance is clearly the strongest bet. They need to leverage their enormous resources, in part to counter technology challenges. It is likely they will need to acquire financial technology companies that are nibbling at their heels.

Insurance has incumbency in its favor, but does not have the heft of banking and finance. It is easy to imagine technology disrupting this

Table 7.1   Innovation Assessment for Gotham

	Innovation Outlook		
	Banking & Finance	*Insurance*	*Media & Publishing*
Strengths	Incumbency	Incumbency	Incumbency
Weaknesses	High Costs & Taxes	High Costs & Taxes	Technology Challenges
Opportunities	Leverage Resources	Leverage Technology	Leverage Brands
Threats	Technology	Technology	Technology

industry, not just in New York City. AI-based insurance underwriting seems inevitable. Complete automation of the industry is conceivable. Players in this market need to get ahead of the game.

Media and publishing provide rich opportunities for growth. Information technologies pervasively affect our lives. Smart televisions, wi-fi networks, computers, and handheld digital devices have transformed our homes into media ecosystems. People desire content tailored to their desires when and where they want it. However, they probably do not want it printed and they would rather not have advertisements.

Streaming services are now dominating, not just for traditional content but also for online games, which have become increasingly sophisticated. We use the same infrastructure for Teams, Webex, and Zoom. Thus, work and play are similarly enabled. Can traditional media and publishing companies prosper in this new environment? They will need a different mindset and new investment priorities.

All three domains need to mitigate the high labor costs and taxes of operating in New York City. This can be accomplished by reducing labor content or relying on labor remote from the city. Both will reduce real estate expenses, which will also reduce city tax revenues.

When I moved from New York City to Washington, DC, in 2017, I reduced my costs of living by 50%. Moving from Washington, DC, to Asheville, NC, in 2024, costs of living were again cut by 50%. However, my clients did not change and the people I worked with remained the same. We were still on Zoom, with in-person meetings every few months.

Epilogue

I have been traveling to New York City for over 60 years, first by train, then plane, and then subway when I lived in Hoboken for almost five years.

Before I moved there, I always found the city overwhelming. Being plopped into a metro area of over 20 million people is disorienting.

My apprehension greatly decreased when I got used to making my way around on subways and buses. I still was occasionally amazed. I was in Manhattan for a breakfast meeting. Walking from the PATH to the meeting, I noticed a sign, Early Bird Special: Parking $35 Per Hour. What would it cost later?

Friday afternoons, particularly in the summer, astounded me as endless cars jostled and honked horns trying to get out of the city, to the Hamptons I supposed. Overall, the city seemed expensive, crazy, and dirty. Was litter ever picked up? Did all the honking horns ever help? Were double parkers ever penalized?

I came to see the city has having two purposes – absorbing immigrants and making money. Immigrants are attracted to the most expensive city in the United States because housing and other benefits are guaranteed. Consequently, roughly one-third of city residents are foreign born.

As discussed earlier in this chapter, the overarching objective in New York City is making money, not by creating tangible value but by identifying small differences between buy and sell prices and exploiting them. Upon spotting a one penny difference, one acquires a billion dollars of this equity, holds it for milliseconds, then sells it for a handsome profit. As everyone does this pervasively, much money is made – but no value is created.

Actually, these behaviors do reflect values – greed, exploitation, and wealth. With the monies they make, these traders buy palatial homes in Westchester Country, much the same as Atlantans buy McMansions in Alpharetta. Both enjoy conspicuous consumption.

There are two notable differences. The wealthy in Gotham want to tell you what they paid for everything. They also want to tell you their net worth and ask about yours. They want to win the race to determine who has the most money.

More broadly, they will tell you exactly what they think about everything, without a thought as to whether or not you will be surprised or embarrassed. To an extent, this can be refreshing, yet there are inevitably some things you just do not want to know.

Chapter 8

Capital

The Algonquian-speaking Piscataway tribe inhabited the lands around the Potomac River when Europeans first arrived and colonized the region in the early 17th century. The Nacotchtank tribe maintained settlements around the Anacostia River. Over time, the tribe was absorbed by Maryland's Piscataway tribe.

In 1632, English fur trader Henry Fleet documented an American Indian village of the Nacotchtank people called Tohoga on the site of present-day Georgetown and established trade there. The area was then part of the Province of Maryland.

George Gordon constructed a tobacco inspection house along the Potomac in approximately 1745. The port city of Alexandria, Virginia, was founded in 1749, and the port of Georgetown was founded in 1751. Georgetown was at the head of navigation (the farthest point upstream that oceangoing boats could navigate) of the Potomac River. Cargo from ocean-going ships would be transferred to barges, or vice versa, at Georgetown to continue up or down the Potomac.

In 1751, the legislature of the Province of Maryland authorized the purchase of 60 acres of land from Gordon and George Beall. A survey of the town was completed in February 1752. Since Georgetown was founded during the reign of George II of Great Britain, some speculate that the town was named after him. Another theory is that the town was named after its founders, George Gordon and George Beall. The Maryland Legislature formally issued a charter and incorporated the town in 1789.

The site was already a tobacco trading post when the inspection house was built. Warehouses, wharves, and other buildings were then constructed

 DOI: 10.4324/9781003507468-8

around the inspection house, and it quickly became a small community. Georgetown grew into a thriving port, facilitating trade and shipments of goods from colonial Maryland. The Old Stone House, built in 1765, in Georgetown is the city's oldest still standing building.

Georgetown University

Jesuit settlers from England founded the Province of Maryland in 1634. In 1646, the defeat of the Royalists in the English Civil War led to stringent laws against Roman Catholic education and the extradition of known Jesuits from the colony. During most of the remainder of Maryland's colonial period, Jesuits conducted Catholic schools clandestinely. It was not until after the end of the American Revolution that plans to establish a permanent Catholic institution for education in the United States were realized.

Due to Benjamin Franklin's recommendation, Pope Pius VI appointed former Jesuit John Carroll as the first head of the Roman Catholic Church in the United States, even though the papal suppression of the Jesuit order was still in effect. Carroll began meetings of local clergy in 1783 near Annapolis, Maryland, where they planned the development of a new university. On January 23, 1789, Carroll finalized the purchase of the property in Georgetown on which Dahlgren Quadrangle was later built. Future Congressman William Gaston was enrolled as the school's first student on November 22, 1791, and instruction began on January 2, 1792.

Forming the District

In July of 1790, Congress passed the Residence Act, which approved the creation of a national capital on the Potomac River. The exact location was to be selected by President George Washington, who signed the bill into law. Formed from land donated by Maryland and Virginia, the initial shape of the federal district was a square measuring 10 miles on each side and totaling 100 square miles. Alexandria and Georgetown were included in the territory.

In 1791 and 1792, a team surveyed the borders of the federal district and placed boundary stones at every mile point; many of these stones are still standing. A new federal city was then constructed on the north bank of the Potomac River, to the east of Georgetown. In 1791, three commissioners overseeing the capital's construction named the city in honor of President Washington.

The federal district was named Columbia, a feminine form of Columbus, which was a fond name for the United States commonly used at that time. In 1800, following the relocation of the nation's capital from Philadelphia, the U.S. Congress began assembling in the newly constructed United States Capitol.

Congress passed the District of Columbia Organic Act of 1801, which officially organized the district and placed the entire territory under the exclusive control of the federal government. The area within the district was organized into two counties, the County of Washington to the east and north of the Potomac and the County of Alexandria to the west and south. After the Act's passage, citizens in the district were no longer considered residents of Maryland or Virginia, which ended their representation in Congress.

Capital Region

The National Capital Region, sometimes referred to as Greater Washington or colloquially as the DMV (named after the District of Columbia, Maryland, and Virginia), is the metropolitan area centered around Washington, DC, the federal capital of the United States.

The metropolitan area is one of the most educated and affluent metropolitan areas in the United States. The metro area anchors the southern end of the densely populated Northeast megalopolis with an estimated total population of over 6.4 million, making it the sixth-largest metropolitan area in the nation.

Wards and Neighborhoods

The District is divided into eight wards, each with approximately 75,000 residents, and each with its own rich history, vibrant neighborhoods, and diverse population, making DC a truly distinct and remarkable city. Each ward is represented on the DC City Council.

Neighborhoods in Washington, DC are distinguished by their history, culture, architecture, demographics, and geography. The names of 131 neighborhoods are unofficially defined by the DC Office of Planning. Washington's local neighborhood history and culture is often presented as being distinct from that of the national government.

JOHNS HOPKINS

Johns Hopkins University is a private research university in Baltimore, Maryland. Founded in 1876, Johns Hopkins was the first US university based on the European research institution model. The university was named for its first benefactor, the American entrepreneur and Quaker philanthropist Johns Hopkins. His $7 million bequest to establish the university was the largest philanthropic gift in US history up to that time. The university revolutionized higher education in the United States by integrating teaching and research.

The Johns Hopkins University School of Medicine was founded in 1893. The School of Medicine shares a campus with Johns Hopkins Hospital and Johns Hopkins Children's Center, established in 1889. The School of Medicine consistently ranks among the top medical schools in the United States in terms of research grants awarded by the National Institutes of Health, and other factors.

The Johns Hopkins Bloomberg School of Public Health is the public health graduate school. Founded in 1916, it is the second independent, degree-granting institution for research in epidemiology and training in public health, and the largest public health training facility in the United States. For the past three decades, the school has been ranked first in public health. The school was renamed in 2001, in honor of Michael Bloomberg for his financial support and commitment to the school.

The Johns Hopkins Applied Physics Laboratory (APL) has served as a major governmental defense contractor since 1942. In tandem with on-campus research, Johns Hopkins has every year since 1979 had the highest federal research funding of any American university. APL itself secures over $1.5 billion in research funding.

The University recently relocated its Washington, DC-based graduate programs to a new, high-visibility home in the heart of the nation's capital. In 2019, the University reached agreement to purchase the iconic building that had housed the Newseum, located on Pennsylvania Avenue, the District's most prestigious thoroughfare. Johns Hopkins has transformed the building into a modern, world-class interdisciplinary academic facility anchored by their School of Advanced International Studies.

Economic Base

The Washington metropolitan area has a GDP of over $560 billion. Federal government expenditures account for over 31% of DC's GDP. It accounts for 2.3% of the nation's GDP. Professional services provided to other than government customers account for almost 25% of DC's GDP.

The metro area has the largest science and engineering workforce of any metropolitan area in the nation ahead of the combined San Francisco Bay Area workforce and Chicago metropolitan area workforce. The metro area was ranked as the second-best high-tech center in the United States, behind Silicon Valley and ahead of the Boston metropolitan area.

Fueling the metropolitan area's ranking was almost 250,000 tech jobs in the region, a total eclipsed only by New York, Los Angeles, and the San Francisco Bay Area, as well as DC having the highest master's or doctoral degree attainment among the 100 ranked metropolitan areas.

Many defense contractors are headquartered in the Washington area near the Pentagon in Arlington. Local defense contractors include BAE Systems Inc. ($23 billion), Boeing ($67 billion), General Dynamics ($39 billion), Leidos ($14 billion), Lockheed Martin ($66 billion), Northrop Grumman ($37 billion), and Raytheon Technologies ($67 billion). Of course, much of this $300+ billion revenue is realized in locales far beyond the DC metro area.

The Washington metropolitan area has a significant biotechnology indus-try. Companies with a major presence in the region include Merck, Pfizer, Human Genome Sciences, Martek Biosciences, and Qiagen. Additionally, many biotechnology companies such as United Therapeutics, Novavax, Emergent BioSolutions, Parabon NanoLabs, and MedImmune have head-quarters in the region.

The telecommunications and tech industry in DC spans a diverse range of players across internet infrastructure, broadcasting, satellite communica-tions, and data centers. Firms headquartered in the area include Cogent Communications, GTT Communications, Hughes Network Systems, iCore Networks, Iridium Communications, Intelsat, Ligado Networks, NII Holdings, Oceus Networks, OneWeb, Tegna Inc., Transaction Network Services, Verisign, WorldCell, and XO Communications.

The media industry is a significant portion of metropolitan Washington's economy with the second-largest concentration of journalists and media personnel in the United States after the New York metropolitan area. The industry's DC presence includes major publications with national audiences such as *The Washington Post*, *U.S. News & World Report*, and *USA Today*, as well as new media publishers such as Vox Media, RealClearPolitics, Axios, and Politico.

More than 74,000 tourism-sector jobs exist in DC. Almost 20 million domestic tourists visit the city annually, and domestic and international tourists combined to spend over $7 billion. The convention industry is also significant, with DC hosting numerous conventions, with an estimated total economic impact of almost $300 million. There were almost 60 million visitors to national parks in the National Capital Region, generating close to $1.6 billion in economic impact.

The Washington metropolitan area contains the headquarters of numerous companies in the hospitality and hotel industries. Major companies with headquarters in the region include Marriott International, The Ritz-Carlton Hotel Company, Hilton Worldwide, Park Hotels and Resorts, Choice Hotels, Host Hotels and Resorts, and HMSHost.

The median net worth for white households in the DC region is $284,000, while the median net worth for Hispanic–Latino households is $13,000, and for African American households is $3,500, clearly illustrating the disparities across the metro area.

Asian Americans have the highest median net worth in the Washington area ($220,000 for Chinese American households, $430,000 for Vietnamese American households, $496,000 for Korean American households, and $573,000 for Indian American households).

Broader Context

As the seat of the federal government, the Capital has no comparable ecosystem in the United States. One might argue that London, Paris, and Rome, for example, could provide interesting comparisons. However, it is more relevant to consider the relations between the Capital and the 50 US states, as well as other countries such as China, India, Israel, Russia, and Ukraine.

Congress includes 100 senators and 435 representatives that serve the interests of the 50 states. There are also 13,000 registered lobbyists, spending $4 billion trying to influence these 535 people. Thus, there are 24 lobbyists per member of Congress, spending $7.5 million per member. The result is a large portfolio of authorizations and appropriations that fund the work of the government.

A significant portion of this work involves relationships with other countries as allies or adversaries, preferably via economic rather than military relationships. There is also consideration of immigration policies, which are laced with political complications. Also of importance are collective actions to address, for example, climate change. Stalemates in addressing issues are common.

Some of this work is accomplished via standing multi-lateral organizations such as the United Nations (UN) and the North Atlantic Treaty Organization (NATO). There are also intergovernmental forums such as the G7 and G20 that provide regular venues for discussions and debates. Of course, there are also many bilateral interactions between countries.

Bodies of Water

DC is bordered on the west by the Potomac River and on the east by the Anacostia River. The Potomac River flows from the Potomac Highlands in West Virginia to the Chesapeake Bay in Maryland. It is 405 miles long, with a drainage area of 14,700 square miles, and is the fourth-largest river along the East Coast of the United States. Over 5 million people live within its watershed.

The Anacostia River flows from Prince George's County in Maryland into Washington, DC, where it ultimately empties into the Potomac River at Buzzard Point. It is about 9 miles long. The name "Anacostia" derives from the area's early history as Nacotchtank, a settlement of Anacostan Native Americans on the banks of the river.

The Chesapeake Bay is the largest estuary in the United States. The Bay is primarily separated from the Atlantic Ocean by the Delmarva Peninsula, including parts of the Eastern Shore of Maryland, the Eastern Shore of Virginia, and the state of Delaware. The Potomac River is one of more than 150 major rivers and streams that flow into the Bay's 64,299-square-mile drainage basin, which covers parts of six states. The Bay is approximately 200 miles long from its northern headwaters in the Susquehanna River to its outlet in the Atlantic Ocean.

Crossing Bodies of Water

Washington DC has seven major bridges across the Potomac River, six major bridges across the Anacostia River, and more than a dozen bridges scattered along the length of Rock Creek Park. Some of these structures are beautiful and provide the city's best views, while others are functional yet indistinct. The capital region has dozens of bridges across small streams, over other streets and highways, and railroad tracks. Washington DC's bridges carry hundreds of thousands of vehicles a day and are important to the region's infrastructure.

There are numerous water taxi services on the Potomac connecting Georgetown, The Wharf, Alexandria, and National Harbor. There are also several Potomac River cruise companies, typically originating in Georgetown. There appears to be limited daily commuting using these water-based services.

Before buses, cars, and the Metro ran through DC, horse-drawn street-cars were the major source of transportation for 19th-century Washingtonians. The first DC line was laid in the summer of 1862. By the 1880s, Washington had five different streetcar companies and ten routes crisscrossing the entire city.

The first streetcar service east of the Anacostia River began in 1877. This fueled rapid residential development, connecting the area to Navy Yard and downtown DC. These early streetcars were horse-drawn, but replaced with electric cars by 1900 and ultimately buses by 1962.

The topographical barrier of Rock Creek Park had hindered development north of Dupont Circle. However, in 1891, the Rock Creek Railway company built the first bridge spanning the park, extending Connecticut Avenue to the newly built Chevy Chase neighborhood. A streetcar line followed in 1892, catalyzing development all along today's Metro Red Line route.

The Washington Metro now serves the Washington metropolitan area. It is administered by the Washington Metropolitan Area Transit Authority (WMATA), which also operates the Metrobus service under the Metro name. Opened in 1976, the network now includes six lines, 98 stations, and 129 miles of route. The Red Line was the first of the six lines. Daily ridership is roughly a half million people, second only to New York City's public transit system.

Higher Education

There are over 200 colleges and universities in the National Capital Region. Many universities from across the United States have a "presence" in the District to facilitate their relationships with a wide range of federal agencies as well as Congress.

In the District

There are several well-known universities in the District. The following eight institutions are listed in order of founding date.

- Georgetown University (1789) is a private Jesuit research university founded by Bishop John Carroll and, as noted earlier, the oldest Roman Catholic institution of higher education in the United States
- George Washington University (1821) is a private university founded by three Baptist ministers and chartered by Congress
- University of District Columbia (1851) is a historically black, urban land-grant institution and the only public University in the nation's capital
- Gallaudet University (1864) is a private federally chartered university for the education of the deaf and hard of hearing, founded as a grammar school for both deaf and blind children
- Howard University (1867) is a private, federally chartered historically black research university and HBCU (Historically Black Colleges and Universities)
- Johns Hopkins University (1876) is a private research university in Baltimore, but also operating in DC, the first US university based on the European research institution model, named for an American entrepreneur and Quaker philanthropist
- Catholic University (1887) is a pontifical university of the Catholic Church in the United States and the only institution of higher education founded by the United States Conference of Catholic Bishops
- American University (1893) is a private Methodist-affiliated institution chartered by Congress

The National Capital Region includes several highly regarded public universities. The University of Maryland in College Park includes top programs in science, technology, engineering, and mathematics (STEM). Virginia has several strong public universities, including George Mason University, Virginia Tech (VT), and the University of Virginia (UVA). George Mason is headquartered in Fairfax, VT in Blacksburg, and UVA in Charlottesville. However, UVA and particularly VT have strong presence in metro DC.

The Virginia Commonwealth's $1 billion investment in higher education, seeding the doubling of existing computer science and computer engineering programs in Blacksburg, Virginia, helped attract Amazon and was the catalyst for launching the Virginia Tech Innovation Campus in Arlington.

Capital Politics

The District of Columbia has limited home rule, allowing for the popular election of a mayor and a city council to four-year terms. The council is empowered to set tax rates, formulate the budget, and organize or abolish any agency of the District's government. Congress, however, retains the right to veto any actions by the District government that threaten "federal interest," and the budgets that are passed by the council and approved by the mayor have to be reviewed and enacted by Congress.

DC has long lobbied for statehood, as has Puerto Rico. This would require a Constitutional Amendment approved by at least 36 states. This would add four Senators and two or more Representatives to Congress, all likely Democrats. Republicans have long done their best to thwart this initiative.

Abolitionist Era

Slavery existed in the nation's capital from the very beginning of the city's history in 1790, when Congress created the federal territory from lands formerly held by the slave states of Virginia and Maryland. Because of its advantageous location between these two states, Washington became a center of the domestic slave trade in the 19th century and was home to one of the most active slave depots in the nation.

During its early years, Georgetown College suffered from considerable financial strain. The Maryland Society of Jesus began its restoration in 1805, and Jesuit affiliation, in the form of teachers and administrators, bolstered confidence in the college. The school relied on private sources of funding and the limited profits from local lands which had been donated to the Jesuits. To raise money for Georgetown and other schools in 1838, Maryland Jesuits conducted a mass sale of some 272 slaves to two Deep South plantations in Louisiana, from their six in Maryland, ending their slaveholding.

In the 1830s, the District's southern territory of Alexandria declined economically due in part to neglect of it by Congress. Alexandria was a major market in the domestic slave trade and pro-slavery residents feared that abolitionists in Congress would end slavery in the District, further depressing the local economy. Alexandria's citizens petitioned Virginia to take back the land it had donated to form the District through a process known as retrocession.

The Virginia General Assembly voted in February 1846 to accept the return of Alexandria. In July 1846, Congress went further, agreeing to return all territory that Virginia had ceded to the district during its formation. This left the district's area consisting only of the portion originally donated by Maryland. Confirming the fears of pro-slavery Alexandrians, the Compromise of 1850 outlawed the slave trade in the District, although not slavery itself. Slavery remained legal in the District until April of 1862, when President Abraham Lincoln signed into law an act abolishing slavery in the District of Columbia, the DC Emancipation Act.

Progressive Era

From the 1890s to the 1920s – the Progressive Era – the United States experienced dramatic social, cultural, and political changes. Confronted with domestic and international challenges, Congress reexamined the government's role in the economy and the environment and the nation's place in the world. President Theodore Roosevelt played a significant role in this process.

Prominent investigative journalists – termed "muckrakers" – and citizen activists pushed Congress to pass landmark legislation, and states ratified new amendments to the Constitution. Sinclair Lewis and Ida Tarbell were among the notable muckrakers. This period of dynamic reform forever altered the democratic process, the everyday lives of all Americans, and the notion of "We the People."

Civil Rights Era

This era has a long history, with many substantial contributors to progress. Most often cited is August of 1963, when a quarter of a million people rallied in Washington, DC, for the "March on Washington for Jobs and Freedom" to demand an end to segregation, fair wages and economic justice, voting rights, education, and long overdue civil rights protections. The event culminated at the Lincoln Memorial, where Dr. Martin Luther King Jr. delivered his famous "I Have a Dream" speech.

The Civil Rights Act of 1964 was signed by President Lyndon Johnson. It guaranteed federal protection under the law for all Americans. The Act protected the right to vote; prohibited discrimination in public accommodations based on race, color, religion, or national origin; outlawed job discrimination based on race, color, religion, sex, or national origin; and gave the federal government broad authority in enforcing the federal laws on the state and the local level. Civil rights acts passed over the remaining 1960s would attempt to essentially end discrimination in every facet of life.

Challenges

All ecosystems have economic, political, and environmental challenges, but the nature of these challenges tends to differ based on the characteristics of the ecosystem.

Economic Challenges

DC is a high cost of living area, including high income and property taxes. The tax base of the city is threatened by the low occupancy of office buildings resulting from the coronavirus pandemic and substantial changes to working from home. This has also substantially reduced revenues for restaurant and retail services, further decreasing tax revenues.

Political Challenges

The DMV region is plagued by traffic congestion, despite excellent public transportation services. This challenge was mitigated by people working from home, but there are now substantial pressures to return to physical presence. There is substantial political opposition to this.

The dysfunctional Congress presents enormous challenges in terms of public skepticism, loss of confidence, and lack of trust. People's expectations of government are very low, sensing that representatives are only focused on campaign funding and reelection.

Statehood for DC continues to be controversial for people who pay the highest per capita taxes in the United States. DC citizens firmly believe that fairness is not relevant to Congress. All that matters is power, control of resources, and thwarting adversaries.

Environmental Challenges

Environmental events can be enormously damaging. Underground assets such as the subways and tunnels are very difficult to fully protect. The average elevation of the District is 150 ft. Alexandria is 39 ft and Georgetown harbor is 141 ft. Sea level rise due to melting Arctic and Antarctic ice caps might eventually exceed these levels. Protecting the city may be a major economic, political, and environmental challenge.

Innovation Outlook

Venture Capital Funding

The National Capital Region has recently secured $5 billion in annual venture capital investment, of which $1.4 billion was invested in DC.

Growth Opportunities

The region is projected to add 1 million new residents over the next 30 years. 75% of the new jobs will be in three areas: professional and business services, educational and health services, and leisure and hospitality. Little growth in federal employment is projected.

Innovation Assessment

Table 8.1 summarizes an assessment of growth opportunities in professional and business services, educational and health services, and leisure and hospitality.

Digital Transformation of Government

The major players in DC will play substantial, lucrative roles in transforming US governmental operations to digital technology. Paper documentation and surrogates like pdfs will be replaced by real digital data. This will lead to computer-based processes for government operations. This will provide a foundation for digital decision support for policy and investment decisions.

There will be many competitors ranging from the large defense contractors, to the big tech companies (e.g., Alphabet, Apple, Microsoft), to software-savvy new entrants with AI, analytics, etc. A winner-takes-all

Table 8.1 Innovation Assessment for Capital

	Innovation Outlook		
	Professional & Business Services	*Education & Health Services*	*Leisure & Hospitality*
Strengths	Incumbency	Incumbency	Incumbency
Weaknesses	Status Quo	Substantial Inequities	Intense Competition
Opportunities	Digital Transformation	Leverage Technology	Leverage Technology
Threats	Defenders of Status Quo	Technology Competitors	Technology Competitors

approach to this procurement makes great sense, but political pressures will dictate that this very large pie be divided into many pieces. The results will likely be substantial integration difficulties, which will drive up costs and stretch delivery timelines.

This transformation will not be easy. Millions of jobs are associated with supporting paper-based analog processes. Enormous savings will be possible and contractors that can enable this will secure huge contracts. However, the stewards of the status quo will be substantial impediments. Of course, these difficulties will yield substantial large revenues to those who are contracted to enable these changes.

Educational Services

Educational technologies will be key enablers of growth in educational services. Central investments are outlined below. Different disciplines will likely address these investments in different ways. We have explored the impacts of change on humanities, medicine, and engineering. We expect that schools of business and law will also face similar challenges. Nevertheless, the investments by discipline may differ significantly. Note that these investments are highly relevant to educational challenges discussed in earlier chapters.

Online Education

All disciplines will necessarily have to entertain greater use of online teaching as the response to the pandemic has prompted. However, disciplines may differ in emphases. Some of these differences will be driven by the differing content employed in the curricula of these differences. Also of great importance will be the extent that face-to-face interactions are central to each discipline and the extent to which these interactions can be technologically mediated.

Interactive Technologies

Advanced technology can enable compelling interactive portrayals of phenomena ranging from chemistry and physics, to human physiology and behaviors, to social and cultural interactions. These interactive technologies can augment reality and provide profound educational experiences. The quality of these immersive portrayals has steadily improved and the costs, at least on widely available platforms, have progressively decreased. The economics of such technologies depend, however, on the number of students across which costs can be amortized.

Knowledge Management

Information access and knowledge management are challenges across disciplines, although the nature of data and knowledge artifacts differ substantially across disciplines. In particular, the technological infrastructure associated with science and technology has benefitted from enormous investments. Humanities have seen important investments and innovations but not at all on the same scale. Of particular note, the data and knowledge artifacts of the humanities were seldom originally created digitally.

Process Improvement

Process modeling and improvement initiatives are significantly affected by two factors. One is the extent to which educational processes are interwoven with operational processes. This is greatest for medicine where much of education happens during delivery of clinical services. In engineering, considerable research happens with industry and undergraduate cooperative education programs are pervasive. Humanities have few similar processes and thus can be approached in a more straightforward manner.

The second factor is scale. When an undergraduate major, for example, electrical, industrial, or mechanical engineering, has well over 1,000 students in one department, technology investments can be amortized across many students and, thereby, justify much greater investments. If such institutions are also well resourced, the human and financial resources can be marshaled to undertake these investments.

Health Services

The future of health innovation will involve seamless information sharing and care coordination. Successful innovators will master these capabilities. Building on this baseline will be remote patient monitoring to transform prevention and chronic disease management. These aspirations are extremely competitive. DC will need to be a leader rather than a follower.

Fortunately, many of the key players are resident in the DC ecosystem, in terms of requirements, regulations, and payment. Successful innovators will be very well connected in this ecosystem, with demonstrated abilities to deliver inventions that predictably transition to market innovations.

A central challenge will involve addressing the highly fragmented nature of the US system for healthcare delivery, particularly if population health is the goal. Population health involves integration of health, education, and social services to keep a defined population healthy, to address health challenges holistically, and to assist with the realities of being mortal.

Integrated delivery of health, education, and social services is greatly complicated in the United States by the separation of providers and payers entangled by a fee-for-services economic model. All of the seams among the fragments of the system are opportunities for profits without actually providing any health-related services. Capitated payments for keeping people healthy, as exemplified by Medicare Advantage, should be a priority. Integration of providers and payers is likely a key to success.

Leisure and Hospitality

Consumers are increasingly expecting integrated leisure and hospitality services. They do not want to separately manage air travel, ground transportation, lodging, food, and entertainment engagements. Digital packaging of leisure and hospitality offerings can increase consumer demand and provide better margins for all the component services.

DC offers a wonderful opportunity to leverage the wealth of leisure and hospitality opportunities in the metro region. Many of these opportunities are free, but complicated to understand and access. Digital packaging can make this much easier and user-friendly. Advanced capabilities for virtual experiences, for example, gamification, can make the planning of experiences compelling. Such planning would likely be online and could occur before people arrive in DC.

A simple example is accessing public transportation. The city's excellent bus and subway system can seem daunting, but once understood is very user-friendly. One can gain this understanding online, including a virtual trip, for instance, from the airport to one's hotel. The subsequent actual experience will then be much less stressful.

Epilogue

Government involves complex webs of laws, regulations, and policies. Laws are enacted by Congress, state legislatures, or city governments. In principle, local laws should not conflict with state laws, and state laws should not conflict with federal laws. Violations of laws can involve criminal penalties, including incarceration and fines.

Regulations are promulgated by executive agencies at federal, state, and local levels. Violations of regulations typically involve fines. Policies are issued at all levels of government. Conflicts with policies are typically handled via management interventions such as budget controls.

The primary cultural values of government include power, control, and patronage (e.g., jobs) rather than money, possessions, and wealth. Money is a means to gaining and retaining power. Control and patronage are perquisites of having power, as illustrated in Chapter 4 for Chicago and Chapter 7 for New York City.

This is not to suggest that power is necessarily corrupting. In other words, worthwhile initiatives often result, leading to positive outcomes. Yet power and control are the means to these ends. Constituencies, and the outcomes they seek, are the forces that determine who ascends to power and control.

Politics and law have precedence over science and engineering. Behavioral and social science will inform what laws, regulations, and policies are acceptable and embraced. Yet technological innovations can serve as seeds for change as we have experienced with the Internet and iPhones.

Chapter 9

Mountains

North Carolina ranges from the highest elevation east of the Mississippi River, at almost 7,000 ft, to an Atlantic coastline that runs 320 miles, second in length to Florida among East Coast states. Charlotte, a hub for banking and financial services, is one of the 25 largest cities in the United States and the largest city in North Carolina.

The Raleigh-Durham-Chapel Hill area of North Carolina is also called the Research Triangle because of its proximity to three major research universities – Duke, the University of North Carolina at Chapel Hill, and North Carolina State University – as well as being a hub for technology and biotech companies.

Thus, North Carolina as a whole is an innovation ecosystem. This chapter focuses on Asheville, the largest city in Western North Carolina, and the state's 11th most populous city. According to the 2020 census, the city's population was 94,589, up from 83,393 in the 2010 census. Asheville is 130 miles west of Charlotte.

The purpose of this focus is to consider innovation at a distance from major metropolitan areas. To an extent, the Mountains are similar to The Island, although the Shining City is only 60 miles distant. People will drive an hour each way to commute to a job, but rarely are willing to drive two hours each way. Consequently, innovation in small, distant cities tends to be more locally focused.

DOI: 10.4324/9781003507468-9

Before the Settlers

Over the course of geological time, the Appalachian Mountains have risen three times due to continental drift and collisions and been weathered down from their peak of nearly 30,000 ft to their current highest elevation of 6,684 ft at Mt. Mitchell. The Great Smoky Mountains are a range within the Appalachians, rising along the Tennessee–North Carolina border in the southeastern United States.

The range is sometimes called the Smoky Mountains and the name is commonly shortened to the Smokies. They are best known as the home of the Great Smoky Mountains National Park, which protects most of the range. The park was established in 1934, and, with over 13 million visits per year, it is the most visited national park in the United States.

In 1914, Edith Vanderbilt sold approximately 86,700 acres of the Biltmore estate's forested mountain land, known as Pisgah Forest, to the federal government, creating the Pisgah National Forest. It is administered by the United States Forest Service, part of the United States Department of Agriculture. The Pisgah National Forest is completely contained within the state of North Carolina.

The Great Smokies is home to an estimated 187,000 acres of old-growth forest, constituting the largest such stand east of the Mississippi River. The cove hardwood forests in the range's lower elevations are among the most diverse ecosystems in North America. The Great Smokies are also home to the densest black bear population in the eastern United States and the most diverse salamander population outside of the tropics.

The name "Smoky" comes from the natural fog that often hangs over the range and presents as large smoke plumes from a distance. This fog is caused by the vegetation emitting volatile organic compounds, chemicals that have a high vapor pressure and easily form vapors at normal temperature and pressure.

The Great Smoky Mountains stretch from the Pigeon River in the northeast to the Little Tennessee River in the southeast. The sources of several rivers are located in the Smokies, including the Little Pigeon River, the Oconaluftee River, and the Little River. Streams in the Smokies are part of the Tennessee River watershed and are thus entirely west of the Eastern Continental Divide.

Around 20,000 years ago, subarctic glaciers advanced southward across North America, and although they never reached the Smokies, the advancing glaciers led to colder mean annual temperatures and an increase in precipitation throughout the range. Trees were unable to survive at the higher elevations and were replaced by tundra vegetation. Spruce-fir forests occupied the valleys and slopes below approximately 4,950 ft. The persistent freezing and thawing during this period created the large blockfields that are often found at the base of large mountain slopes.

Between 16,500 and 12,500 years ago, the glaciers to the north retreated and mean annual temperatures rose. The tundra vegetation disappeared, and the spruce-fir forests retreated to the highest elevations. Hardwood trees moved into the region from the coastal plains, replacing the spruce-fir forests in the lower elevations. The temperatures continued warming until around 6,000 years ago, when they began to gradually grow cooler.

Early Settlers

Before the arrival of the Europeans, the land where Asheville now exists was within the boundaries of the Cherokee Nation. In 1540, the expedition of Spanish explorer Hernando de Soto visited the area.

The first European settlement in North Carolina was a small Spanish fort located in present-day Burke County near Morganton, about 60 miles east of Asheville. Captain Juan Pardo built Fort San Juan in 1567 in the Native American town of Joara. Fort San Juan was built nearly 20 years before the English "Lost Colony" at Roanoke Island and 40 years before the Jamestown settlement.

After 1588, a weaker Spain had not the resources to respond to English settlement, and with little resistance from other European powers, England claimed North Carolina. The Spaniards failed to settle the eastern seaboard of North America, north of Florida, due to a lack of resources, a hostile environment, and resistance from Native Americans.

The Province of Carolina became a province of the Kingdom of England and later the Kingdom of Great Britain when it was chartered in North America in 1663. Northern Carolina, like Rhode Island in the North, drew the region's discontented masses, as discussed in Chapter 2. As the northern and southern locales of Carolina evolved separately and as their differing geographies and inhabitants steered contrasting courses, calls for a formal split emerged. In 1712, North Carolina and South Carolina became distinct colonies.

When the first white settlers reached the Great Smoky Mountains in the late 1700s they found themselves in the land of the Cherokee Indians. The tribe, one of the most culturally advanced on the continent, had permanent towns, cultivated croplands, sophisticated political systems, and extensive networks of trails. Most of the Cherokee were forcibly removed in the 1830s to Oklahoma in a tragic episode known as the Trail of Tears.

Cherokee is a town on the reservation home of the Eastern Band of the Cherokee Nation, in western North Carolina. At Oconaluftee Indian Village, the 18th-century Cherokee lifestyle is preserved via live demonstrations. In summer at the outdoor Mountainside Theatre, the drama "Unto These Hills" tells the tribal story. The nearby Great Smoky Mountains National Park features campgrounds and Appalachian hiking trails.

Life for the early European settlers was primitive, but by the 1900s there was little difference between the mountain people and their con-temporaries living in rural areas beyond the mountains. Earlier settlers had lived off the land by hunting the wildlife, utilizing the timber for buildings and fences, growing food, and pasturing livestock in the clear-ings. As the decades passed, many areas that had once been forest became fields and pastures. People farmed, attended church, hauled their grain to the mill, and maintained community ties in a typically rural fashion.

The agricultural pattern of life in the Great Smoky Mountains changed with the arrival of lumbering in the early 1900s. Within 20 years, the largely self-sufficient economy of the people here was almost entirely replaced by dependence on manufactured items, store bought food, and cash. Logging boom towns sprang up overnight.

Loggers were rapidly cutting the great primeval forests that remained on these mountains. Unless the course of events could be quickly changed, there would be little left of the region's special character and wilderness resources. Intervention came when the Great Smoky Mountains National Park was established in 1934. The forest was saved, at least the 20% that remained uncut within park boundaries.

More than 1,200 landowners had to leave their land once the park was established. They left behind many farm buildings, mills, schools, and churches. Over 70 of these structures have since been preserved so that Great Smoky Mountains National Park now contains the largest collection of historic log buildings in the East.

Evolution of Asheville

After the American Revolution, Colonel Samuel Davidson and his family received a land grant from the state of North Carolina to settle in the Swannanoa Valley in the Blue Ridge Mountains. The Davidsons lived on Christian Creek in the Swannanoa Valley area known as "Eden Land." This early settlement in 1785 paved the way for the future of what would become the city of Asheville.

On November 21, 1789, North Carolina was granted statehood. It was the 12th of the original 13 states to join the Union. Rhode Island was the 13th on May 29, 1790.

In 1792, Buncombe County was established with a city called "Morristown" as its county seat. In 1797, that city was renamed Asheville after North Carolina Governor Samuel Ashe. As a city in the Blue Ridge Mountains, Asheville was an outpost in 1797.

What became Asheville primarily served as a crossroads of Indian trails on a plateau surrounded by mountains and rivers on all sides. When William Oliver Wolfe arrived in 1880, the city still only contained a little over 2,600 permanent residents.

The Western North Carolina Railroad, which had begun in Salisbury, NC, in 1875, crossed the Eastern Continental Divide and the first train pulled into Asheville on October 2, 1880. The arrival of the railroad transformed Asheville and Buncombe County into a resort and therapeutic health center. Asheville became a hub for visitors searching for a mountain escape, its population climbing to 10,000 permanent residents in 1890.

"Land of the Sky" is a slogan applied to the Mountain region of western North Carolina, and Asheville in particular. It was adopted from the title of a novel, "*The Land of the Sky*"; or *Adventures in Mountain By-Ways* (1876), written by Frances Christine Fisher Tiernan (1846–1920), a native of Salisbury, under the pen name Christian Reid.

George Vanderbilt, grandson of famed shipping entrepreneur and industrialist Cornelius "the Commodore" Vanderbilt, first visited Asheville, North Carolina, in 1888. Captivated by the area's natural beauty, he slowly began purchasing land, ending up with 125,000 acres for what would become his country estate in 1895.

Asheville is called the Paris of the South. With the arrival of the Vanderbilts, tourism jumped and helped steer the city into a prosperous era that saw a number of Art Deco buildings go up downtown, many of which still exist today and have been transformed into shops, restaurants, and bars that give the walkable city a bustling feel – a crucial Parisian element.

By 2020, the population of the city had grown to almost 95,000, as noted earlier, and the metro area to 470,000. Over the 2000–2020 period, the city population has grown by 37% and the metro area by 27%. Migration to Asheville is driven by the natural environment, mild weather, and much lower costs of living compared to most major US cities.

Districts and Neighborhoods

Asheville is composed of several districts and neighborhoods. The city's 46 square miles is 68% of the area of Capital, with 13% of the population. Downtown Asheville is filled with indie boutiques, cutting-edge galleries, and specialty food stores, plus artisan shops in the elegant Grove Arcade. Farm-to-table and Southern restaurants dot the area, alongside breweries, chic cocktail bars, and storied music venues. Eclectic attractions include the Asheville Pinball Museum and the Basilica of Saint Lawrence, with its vast domed ceiling.

The River Arts District is a creative hub along the French Broad River. Former warehouses and mills, many with colorful exterior murals, contain glassblowing, pottery, and other artisan studios, plus indie art galleries. The buzzing dining and nightlife scene encompasses hip cafes, BBQ restaurants, craft breweries, and cozy, chilled-out music venues like the long-running Grey Eagle.

West Asheville is a hip residential area encompassing the Bear Creek, Burton Street, and Hall Fletcher neighborhoods. West Asheville is known for small shops selling vintage clothing, books, and records. Haywood Road is lined with breweries, retro-cool music venues, busy brunch spots, and innovative eateries serving elevated Southern dishes. Carrier Park and French Broad River Park are popular for picnicking, hiking, and river views.

Set in wooded hills, upscale Grove Park-Sunset features striking architecture, including Tudor Revival and Prairie-style homes and the rustic, stone Omni Grove Park Inn, a landmark 1913 hotel with a golf course. Grovewood Village contains the Antique Car Museum, craft studios, galleries, and a modern sculpture garden, plus the Biltmore Industries Homespun Museum, which traces the village's origins as a weaving hub.

The affluent Montford Area Historic District features distinctive Queen Anne, Arts and Crafts, and Colonial Revival houses, many restored as B&Bs.

Each summer, the Montford Park Players bring crowds to Hazel Robinson Amphitheatre for the outdoor Shakespeare Festival. Authors Thomas Wolfe and O. Henry are among those buried in the sprawling Riverside Cemetery, which has flower gardens and statue-topped mausoleums.

Encompassing the Grace and Lakeview Park neighborhoods, North Asheville is a mainly residential area strewn with casual, locally owned restaurants and bistros. Leafy streets are lined with homes in eclectic architectural styles, from midcentury ranch to Tudor Revival. A popular spot for fishing, boating, and paddleboarding, Beaver Lake has waterside paths and a peaceful bird sanctuary with a boardwalk trail.

Economic Base

Innovations in The Mountains are rather different than in the other ecosystems. First of all, a metropolitan area of only 500,000 people differs substantially from six of the other ecosystems. The Island has an even smaller population, but is embedded in the enormous population base of a major metropolitan area.

The Asheville region is a diverse $24 billion economy. Key economic drivers include steady population growth, manufacturing, healthcare, and hospitality. To a great extent, The Mountains are on their own. They cannot depend on an Atlanta, Boston, Chicago, New York, Washington, Amsterdam, London, or Paris.

This represents both a challenge and an opportunity. There is no major economic entity that one can feed upon. Yet people can innovate in ways unique to their particular geographic and economic conditions. Innovations in the small are broadly celebrated.

Asheville is steeped in equal parts artsy innovation and Appalachian tradition. Drawing inspiration and ingredients from its lushly forested, river-veined landscape and a confluence of indigenous, African diaspora, and immigrant cultures, this small city dishes up a flavor as unique and colorful as its heritage. Wild ingredients like ramps and mushrooms foraged in the mountains for thousands of years mingle today on local menus with endless variations on Southern Appalachian staples such as cornbread, pole beans, apple butter, pork belly, sorghum, and other staples that comprised the Southern Appalachian diet.

Local chefs take pride in maintaining time-honored mountain cooking practices like pickling, fermenting, smoking, and drying alongside

BLUE RIDGE PARKWAY

The idea was born when President Franklin Roosevelt visited the newly constructed Skyline Drive in Virginia in 1933. Senator Harry Byrd of Virginia suggested to the president the road should be extended to connect with the recently established Great Smoky Mountains National Park. Roosevelt convened the governors of Virginia, North Carolina, and Tennessee and asked that a planning team be created. In November 1933, this "park-to-park" highway as a public works project was approved.

The decision was met with great controversy, particularly by Asheville. The Chamber of Commerce and other city leaders joined forces to lobby in favor of a road that passed through their city. By the beginning of World War II, approximately 170 miles were open to travel and another 160 miles were under construction. By the mid-1950s, all parkway construction, with the exception of 7.7 miles at Grandfather Mountain, had been completed. It took until 1987 for the Blue Ridge Parkway to be completed and provide a continuous 469-mile route.

The parkway, which is America's longest linear park, runs through 29 counties in Virginia and North Carolina, linking Shenandoah National Park to Great Smoky Mountains National Park. Virginia hosts mile zero to 217 and North Carolina hosts mile 217 to 469. The parkway is the most visited unit of the National Park System. Almost 16 million people visit the parkway annually.

cutting-edge culinary techniques. Paired with the deep collaborative relationships restaurants nurture with the region's thriving community of small, family-owned farms, the end result is food with an unmistakably delicious Asheville terroir.

Asheville's creative vibe and collaborative spirit have fueled the rapid growth of a thriving, eclectic restaurant scene. This small city has a remarkably large pool of talented chefs who source inspiration — as well as market-fresh ingredients — from the region's tight-knit network of innovative farmers, foragers, and food artisans. Appalachian fare, Southern comfort food, and barbecue mingle with flavors from Asia, Europe, the Americas, and beyond, making for a wealth of choices at mealtime.

Overall Economy

As noted above, the Asheville region is a diverse $24 billion economy. Visitors to Asheville spent $2.2 billion in 2019, which generated $3.3 billion in total business sales, including indirect and induced impacts. Tourism-sustained jobs generated a total income of $881 million in 2019 up from $840 million in 2017.

According to the Economic Development Coalition for Asheville-Buncombe County, Mission Health, an independent hospital, was named by Thomas Reuters as one of the top 15 best health systems in the country. Mission Health is also Asheville's largest employer, providing over 8,000 jobs. Its acquisition by HCA in 2019 has recently resulted in a range of profit seeking reductions of service, resulting in workforce and community complaints.

Of course, healthcare in Asheville inherently faces the challenges being experienced nationally. Profit seeking within our highly fragmented delivery system needs significant transformation to enable robust population health for everyone.

Broader Context

Asheville is a small southern city, distant from a major metro area. Metro Atlanta (6.1 million people) is 200 miles south of Asheville. Metro Charlotte (2.7 million) is 130 miles east of Asheville. Metro Nashville (1.3 million) is 300 miles west of Asheville. Asheville is clearly far beyond the exurbs of these metro areas.

Other contrasts include metro Chattanooga (430,000), Savannah (340,000), and Charlottesville (250,000), which are smaller than metro Asheville (500,000) and all quite distant. These small southern cities are also distant from major metro areas in the sense that a daily commute to the closest major metro area would not make sense.

Consequently, Asheville and these other small cities have to establish and cultivate their own identities. Chattanooga has leveraged Civil War history. Savannah thrives on mystery stories and extols the Savannah College of Art and Design. Charlottesville hosts the historic campus of the University of Virginia.

Asheville has the glories of nature, vibrant arts and gustatory delights, and the Art Deco legacy of the Biltmore Estate. It is a city where one can relax and reflect. People are not in a hurry. Ambition can wait or likely has already taken its due in some other ecosystem. Nevertheless, there are expectations that you will listen, talk, laugh, and be an involved citizen.

Bodies of Water

Asheville lakes are stunning – especially because those gorgeous mountains wrap around them – and they provide endless recreational activities. Located directly in Asheville, one can find lakes with Christmas light displays, a bird sanctuary, and the best sunsets.

Asheville's vibrant urban scene, gorgeous mountains, and cultural treasures may be what draws so many visitors to the area, but the French Broad River is arguably what allowed all these things to emerge. The river that flows through Asheville helped shape the Appalachian Mountains.

The French Broad River traverses the states of North Carolina and Tennessee. It flows north 218 miles from near the town of Rosman (near Lake Toxaway) into Tennessee, where its confluence with the Holston River at Knoxville forms the beginning of the Tennessee River.

This ancient river is believed to be the third oldest in the world, around 250 million years old. It is one of the few rivers that flows north. Other notable rivers that flow north are the River Nile in Africa and the St. Johns River in Florida.

Crossing Bodies of Water

There are 395 bridges in Asheville. A dozen of these bridges cross the French Broad River. Before Pearson's Bridge was constructed around 1893, ferries were used to cross the river. Limited water-based capacities for west–east transport resulted in rail and trucks dominating.

Higher Education

The University of North Carolina at Asheville is the largest public institution of higher education. Offerings are limited compared to major campuses. Art students can earn a BA or BFA. Chemistry students can earn a BS or BA. Engineering students spend two years here and then two years at NC State.

It is interesting that arts, science, and technology are better supported than other majors. This is very consistent with the growth opportunities discussed below. UNC Asheville offers free tuition for all in-state students whose families earn less than $80,000 annually.

Other local institutions include Brevard College, Mars Hill University, Montreat College, South College at Asheville, and Warren Wilson College. These long-established colleges tend to emphasize broad liberal educations rather than STEM (science, technology, engineering, and mathematics) as noted above.

Mountain Politics

Asheville is in Buncombe County, NC. *The Buncombe County Strategic Plan 2020-2025* is rather impressive. It starts with their vision. "Buncombe County is a caring community in harmony with its environment where citizens succeed, thrive, and realize their potential."

The mission statement follows:

> We promote a healthy, safe, well-educated, and thriving community with a sustainable quality of life. We provide effective and efficient government our citizens can trust. We deliver needed service through a responsive workforce committed to excellence, integrity, and teamwork.

They articulate core values:

- Respect
- Integrity
- Collaboration
- Honesty
- Equity

Finally, they outline Community Focus Areas:

- Educated and capable community
- Environmental and energy stewardship
- Resident well-being
- Vibrant economy

I have written several books on strategic thinking and planning. I have facilitated scores of strategic planning initiatives in industry, government, and academia. Few of these initiatives have produced such a cogent and compelling framework as outlined above. I know Asheville pretty well, and this articulation fits the city.

Abolitionist Era

Not surprisingly, Asheville has significant baggage from the practice of slavery. In 1850, there were 3.2 million enslaved people of a total population in southern states of 9.6 million. In 1860 there were 4 million enslaved people of a total of 12.2 million. Thus 33.3% of the southern population was enslaved in 1850 and 32.8% in 1860.

In 1850 Buncombe County had 1,717 slaves and 107 free blacks. The total population was 13,425. In 1860, Buncombe County had 1,907 slaves and 283 slave owners. There were 111 free blacks. The total population was 12,654. Thus, slaves accounted for 12.8% in 1850 and 15% in 1860.

Thus, Asheville relied on slavery much less than the south in general. This likely reflected less reliance on plantation economies in Asheville. Nevertheless, lawyer, legislator, and planter Nicholas W. Woodfin owned 122 slaves in Buncombe County, the most owned by anyone. He acquired extensive acreage in the French Broad Valley and likely his slaves were employed on these properties.

The use of slave labor was an important part of Asheville's growing tourism industry. Slave owners in Buncombe County often used slaves to help with their businesses, including hotels. James McConnell Smith owned one of the first hotels in Asheville, the Buck Hotel, often called Smith's Hotel. The use of "servants" in the hotel was advertised, as was the policy of "children and servants" of those who stayed there being charged "two thirds price."

The sale of slaves generally took place on the property of the seller or recently deceased, including many estate sales. A few sales of slaves did occur at the Buncombe County Court House, generally as an estate sale. Only two of these types of sales have been documented from 1850 to 1863.

Progressive Era

Progressives sought to address the problems caused by rapid industrialization, urbanization, immigration, and political corruption and by the enormous concentration of industrial ownership in monopolies. Asheville, it appears, was less concerned with these issues than with economic opportunities, especially for increased tourism.

With the arrival of the Vanderbilts in the late 1800s, tourism jumped and helped steer the city into a prosperous era that saw a number of Art Deco buildings go up downtown, many of which still exist today and have been transformed into shops, restaurants, and bars that give the walkable city a bustling feel.

Kevin Frazier in "Outsiders in the Land of the Sky" in the *Journal of Appalachian Studies* (1998) reported that

> In 1921, Asheville adopted professional city planning in hopes of encouraging economic expansion through improved sanitation, reduce traffic congestion, parks expansion, and land use controls. Of the Southern cities that engaged planners, many soon backed away from planning because of tension between individual interests and government control. Such was not the case with Asheville.

Civil Rights Era

Greensboro, NC, is most widely recognized for the four Black students from the Agricultural & Technical College of North Carolina (now North Carolina A&T State University) who challenged segregationists and set the standard for sit-in movements throughout the state and nation.

In February 1960, four friends sat down at a lunch counter in Greensboro. That may not sound like a legendary moment, but it was. The four people were African American, and they sat where African Americans were not allowed to sit. They did this to take a stand against segregation.

Patrick Parker in *Appalachian Activists: The Civil Rights Movement in Asheville, NC* (2016) observed that

> The story of Asheville's Civil Rights Movement involved slow change. From 1917 to 1965, members of Asheville's black community led a peaceful movement to bring about racial equality in their town. Throughout this almost 50 year endeavor, these civil rights activists successfully furthered the social and political standing of Asheville's black community by employing a unique negotiation strategy that was influenced by opportunities provided by their city's burgeoning tourism industry.

Following the U.S. Supreme Court's decision on *Brown v. Board of Education* in 1954 and subsequent rulings, Asheville's public parks, community centers, pools, and golf courses were no longer officially associated with individual races. However, the school system would not begin full-scale integration until a decade later.

In 1964, the Buncombe County Board of Education adopted a formal four-year plan for integration. The new plan, the first time the board had established a timetable for ending segregation, called for gradual integration, starting in elementary schools and leading to full integration in county high schools by the 1967–1968 school year.

Good intentions, slowly but steadily pursued, seem to have been a hallmark of Asheville's approach to civil rights. There have been occasional protests, bordering on riots, but nothing comparable to the experiences of other cities. It seems to me that addressing poverty using the strategy framework outlined above could go a long way to mitigating inherent frustrations and impatience.

Challenges

All ecosystems have economic, political, and environmental challenges, but the nature of these challenges tends to differ based on the characteristics of the ecosystem.

Political Challenges

Asheville's 90,000-plus population is about 78% white, 12% black, and 5.5% Hispanic. For the four-county Asheville Metropolitan Statistical Area (Buncombe, Haywood, Madison, and Henderson Counties), the population is 84.5% white, 7.2% Hispanic, 4.8% black, 1.3% Asian, and 0.32% American Indian.

Asheville is still fairly segregated as far as where people live. It has become somewhat better, but it is still not the inter-racial haven some would argue. This is further complicated by increasing homelessness. Addressing these disparities, as noted above, will likely be easier in Asheville than in Atlanta, Baltimore, and Washington, DC. Perhaps Asheville could be seen as a "laboratory" for addressing such issues.

Asheville has been characterized as a blue dot in a red or perhaps purple sea. Conservatives in North Carolina have not been happy.

Consequently, gerrymandering by the conservative state legislature has effectively eliminated Asheville's congressional seat. Now two seats divide the city, each of which is roughly 50% liberal and 50% conservative. As a result, one Democratic congressman was replaced by two Republican congressmen. Reversing this will require more legislative liberals.

Economic Challenges

A drop in Asheville tourism during the pandemic hurt local businesses across the board, from shops and restaurants to hotels, bed and breakfasts, and even short-term rentals, as owners and managers faced declining revenue and uncertainty about their finances. This aspect of the economy has of late bounced back.

Anticipated strong population growth will create demands for more affordable housing. This, in turn, will foster pressures on land use. Asheville needs to preserve farmland and implement land use strategies. A city that prides itself on many farm-to-table restaurants must limit the thoughtless conversion of farmland into suburbs.

Fortunately, North Carolina is attractive from a tax perspective. The corporate income tax rate is currently 2.5%. According to the Tax Foundation, for states with corporate tax rates, this is the lowest corporate flat tax rate in the country. North Carolina's sales tax rate is 4.75%, while most of the other ecosystems' rates are near 10% or more. With local taxes, the total sales tax rate for Buncombe County is 7% (Haywood County 7%, Henderson County 6.75%, and Madison County 6.75%).

Environmental Challenges

The changing climate has already made Asheville's weather more unpredictable. The city can expect more extreme heat and excessive rain. Increasing development in the area means more pollution of rivers and roads. Key stakeholders, acting now, need to prepare Asheville for the future the city's citizens hope to live.

The two biggest air quality problems in North Carolina are ground-level ozone (the main ingredient in "smog") and particle pollution. Both pollutants are caused mainly by emissions from cars and trucks, and from the coal-burning power plants that supply a large amount of the city's electricity. Low emission vehicles and power plants will mitigate these problems over time.

Precipitation and heat risk in Asheville are extreme. Drought risk is high. About 15% of buildings in Asheville are at risk of flooding, and the risk level for these buildings is high. About 28% of buildings in Asheville are at risk of wildfire, but the risk level for these buildings is relatively low. Weather challenges, precipitated by the warming climate, will need to be addressed.

On the plus side, sea level rise due to melting ice caps is highly unlikely to affect Asheville with its 2,134-foot elevation.

Innovation Outlook

Venture Capital Funding

Asheville has reported $1.6 billion in capital investments, which is significant in a $24 billion economy and comparable to $4.3 billion for North Carolina as a whole, as well as $4 billion for New South. Nevertheless, these amounts are modest compared to Gotham and Shining City.

Growth Opportunities

The top growth opportunities for Asheville include, with incumbent enterprises noted:

- Advanced manufacturing – GE Aviation, Advanced Manufacturing Solutions Inc., Eaton Corporation
- Science & technology – AvL Technologies, The Elumenati, American Recycling, FLS Energy
- Healthcare – Park Ridge Health, Asheville Specialty Hospital, CarePartners, Mission Health, Mercy Urgent Care, Pardee Hospital, Charles George Veterans Affairs Medical Center
- Education – Asheville City Schools, ArtSpace Charter School, Francine Delany New School for Children, The Learning Community School, Asheville School, Christ School, UNC Asheville
- Small Business – entrepreneurs motivated by Biltmore Estate, Grove Park Inn, and the Western NC Nature Center

Other than healthcare and education, these ventures do not need to generate thousands of jobs. Indeed, enormous workforce needs would be difficult to satisfy. Instead, a slow steady growth in advanced manufacturing, science, and technology would be more likely to be feasible. The Mountains can pioneer its own path.

Innovation Assessment

Table 9.1 summarizes an assessment of growth opportunities in health and education, advanced manufacturing, science, and technology.

There are strong incumbents in health and education services, yet they suffer from nationwide deficiencies imposed by fragmented delivery systems in the United States. Digital transformation of these service ecosystems is urgently needed and ongoing across the United States. Asheville needs to align with and exploit these initiatives.

Asheville has seen strong recent growth in manufacturing. It will be a challenge to scale this success, although one or two new commitments like the recent GE aviation expansion would provide confidence that scaling is achievable. Growth in this area will require strong leveraging of technologies, as competitors will be pursuing this as well.

Growth in science and technology can be centered on climate and sustainability in part because of ongoing strong growth in this area, but also because this orientation has long been central to Asheville's culture. The City of Asheville is getting closer to reaching 100% renewable energy by 2030.

The mountain region provides a readily available lab. There are a large number of green advocacy organizations focused on the direct sustainability

Table 9.1   Innovation Assessment for Mountains

	Innovation Outlook		
	Health & Education Services	*Advanced Manufacturing*	*Science & Technology*
Strengths	Incumbency in Region	Strong Recent Growth	Climate & Sustainability Efforts
Weaknesses	Recent Trends	Achieving Scale	Achieving Scale
Opportunities	Digital Transformation	Leverage Technology	Leverage Partners
Threats	Defenders of Status Quo	Technology Competitors	Science Competitors

of the city and region. These organizations could benefit from strategic alliances with national and international organizations, perhaps those interested in leveraging the Asheville lab.

Innovation Hubs

Henry Doss, in *Forbes* (2016), provides an interesting assessment

> So are science, and technology, and entrepreneurialism, and venture capital, and risk, and vision, and social good, and ... well, just about every ingredient you need for a decidedly innovative and human-centered culture. In fact, it's not at all far-fetched to think of this small city, nestled in the Blue Ridge mountains of North Carolina, as an emerging Silicon Valley. Or, quite possibly, the city is creating a new model of how innovation cultures can operate in the 21st century.

> Nowhere is this emergent innovation and vision more apparent than at The Collider, Asheville's newly opened research, commercialization, and meeting space dedicated to bringing together science, innovation, and business to solve climate challenges. More than a meeting space, more than an incubator or accelerator, The Collider is really an idea made manifest, a physical place and a real and virtual network for "strategic collisions" to occur between business and science. It is an idea that is going to introduce dreams to the world.

> We tend to see things like climate change as problems, or as threats or as something to be fixed. But in the time-honored tradition of innovation – that is, innovation as a force for positive change in the world – the community that is emerging around The Collider sees climate change as an opportunity, one that can put this growing network of climate innovators and scientists smack in the middle of a growing $1 trillion dollar industry. It is an opportunity to both establish Asheville's national reputation for innovation and – more importantly, of course – to simply make the world a better place. It is the latter outcome that will ultimately distinguish The Collider and its many supporters and collaborators from other efforts.

Observation

Mountains and The Island are the two smallest ecosystems in terms of population and area. Interestingly, they bookend the reports on the other six ecosystems to demonstrate that size is not the only success factor.

A significant difference is that The Island is embedded in a large metropolitan region, while Mountains are not. The Island is also dominated by a large government organization while The Mountains are not.

Consequently, Mountains are much more on their own. Their aspirations focus much more on *their* world than the wider world. They want to innovate in ways that benefit their own community. Of course, the Asheville community is attuned to this as well. It is a topic that frequently arises in pubs, bookstores, and elsewhere.

Their goals, plans, and actions are inherently much more human centered than the aspirations of the other ecosystems. They want to understand and benefit all stakeholders. A by-product may be that some people become wealthy, but that is not the overarching goal.

It strikes me that local innovations in Asheville will eventually connect to local innovations elsewhere and, over time, connect to networks of local innovations. This could create bottom-up innovation engines that have broader and higher consequence impacts. Bottom-up coalitions can create very resilient and creative networks.

Epilogue

95% of Asheville residents were born in the United States; 46% were born in North Carolina. The median age is 40. An interesting contrast is Laguna Beach, California. 88% of Laguna Beach residents were born in the United States; 50% were born in California. The median age in Laguna is 51.

The median income in Asheville is $30K; it is $62K for Laguna. The average rent in Ashville is $1,700; it is $3,100 for Laguna. Thus, rent takes roughly the same percentage of income in both resort cities. The population of Asheville is 94,000 in 46 square miles; it is 23,000 for Laguna in 10 square miles. Thus, population densities are commensurate.

Asheville has 11 million annual visitors; Laguna has 6 million. Asheville provides access to over 800 square miles of the Great Smoky Mountains National Park – the most visited national park in the United States.

Laguna provides access to the Pacific Ocean with 64 million square miles but few hiking trails.

People travel to Asheville for nature, arts, food and drink, and hospitality in general. Having been to Laguna many times, I know this seaside city has similar attractions. People move to Asheville for these attractions plus a modest cost of living and low taxes. The same cannot be said for California.

Chapter 10

Contrasts

The overall story is rather similar across ecosystems. Ambitious immigrants arrived, displaced native populations, and proceeded to develop and exploit the geography of their ecosystem, which included leveraging water resources for transportation, commerce, irrigation, etc. They often invented the means of development and exploitation, including unfortunately slavery, but also various technical methods, tools, and devices. Inventions that became innovations enabled industries, revenues, and profits and economic growth, initially for the ecosystem and then more broadly.

Sources of Immigrants

The early immigrants were mostly from Europe. This has substantially changed over the past century. Immigrants from Mexico have been the most numerous for the past half century. Most recently, immigrants to the United States are more likely to come from Asia, especially India and China.

- The Island – English
- Shining City – English
- Heartland – Germans
- Old Country – Germans, Celts
- New South – English, Scots

DOI: 10.4324/9781003507468-10

- Gotham – Dutch
- Capital – German, Scandinavians
- Mountains – English
- Many immigrants came from other, older states

Natives Displaced

Native Americans were displaced by the immigrants, either by disease or violence. Bison, sea cows, and passenger pigeons were among the animal species hunted to extinction. Nine-tenths of the old-growth forests that were expansive over the United States were burned, logged, and cleared away.

- The Island – Narragansetts
- Shining City – Wampanoags
- Heartland – Illiniweks
- Old Country – Paleolithic and Mesolithic groups
- New South – Muscogees and Cherokees
- Gotham – Lenapes
- Capital – Piscataway
- Mountains – Cherokees

Displaced natives and enslaved Africans are central to the American story. We have amended the US Constitution and enacted a range of laws intended to end such exploitation and create a society that reflects the honored values of the Declaration of Independence and the Constitution. This very much remains a work in progress.

Role of Geography

My overarching hypothesis is that geography really matters in terms of natural resources, human capital, and governance. The Island could not dominate agriculture and Heartland could not dominate maritime. Yet, Old Country, which is smaller than Maryland, is a dominant global exporter of agricultural products. So, there is a range of driving forces and success factors, not just geography.

One reason geography enormously matters, historically at least, is access to water for transport of people and goods. The eight ecosystems include 20 rivers that lead to the Gulf of Mexico, the North Sea, and the Atlantic Ocean.

- The Island
  - Narragansett Bay, Sakonnet River, Atlantic Ocean
- Shining City
  - Charles River, Mystic River, Neponset River, Atlantic Ocean
- Heartland
  - Lake Michigan, Mississippi River, Ohio River, Illinois River, Gulf of Mexico
- Old Country
  - Rhine River, Meuse River, Scheldt River, North Sea
- New South
  - Chattahoochee River, Gulf of Mexico, Savannah River, Atlantic Ocean
- Gotham
  - Hudson River, East River, Long Island Sound, Atlantic Ocean
- Capital
  - Potomac River, Chesapeake Bay, Atlantic Ocean
- Mountains
  - French Broad River, Tennessee River, Mississippi River, Gulf of Mexico

As shown in Figure 10.1, the Atlantic Ocean, Gulf of Mexico, and North Sea receive the waters of these 20 rivers. Further, the Gulf of Mexico and the North Sea eventually contribute to the North Atlantic Ocean. I found it surprising that everything eventually ends up in one place, albeit a 16 million square mile place, an area four times the size of the United States.

Figure 10.1   Water flows from all eight ecosystems to the Atlantic Ocean.

Markets Served

Table 10.1 summarizes the primary markets served by each ecosystem. There are significant overlaps, although some ecosystem's markets may be more regional than national. Gotham serves seven of the ten markets, while The Island serves only two. All the other ecosystems serve three or four markets.

Ecosystem of Ecosystems

How about the ecosystem of all eight ecosystems? Table 10.2 summarizes the producer–consumer relationships across the eight ecosystems, that is, the extent to which they serve each other. This table considers such relationships in more detail in terms of products, services, and people. Thus, the dependencies among ecosystems are more nuanced than simply yes or no. They nurture each other in various ways.

Table 10.1 Markets Served by the Eight Ecosystems

	The Island	Shining City	Heartland	Old Country	New South	Gotham	Capital	Mountains
Aerospace & Defense	√	√			√	√	√	
Agriculture & Equipment			√	√				
Arts & Entertainment		√				√	√	√
Automotive & Manufacturing			√					
Banking & Finance						√		
Energy Extraction						√		
Health Sciences		√			√	√	√	
Supply Chain Management			√	√	√	√		
Sustainable Systems			√	√				√
Tourism & Travel	√	√		√		√	√	√

Table 10.2 Producer–Consumer Relationships across the Eight Ecosystems

Producers	Consumers							
	The Island	Shining City	Heartland	Old Country	New South	Gotham	Capital	Mountains
The Island	X	P					M, T	
Shining City		X					E, M, P, T	
Heartland		A, P	X		A, P	A	A, M	
Old Country		A, S		X	A, S	A, S	A, S	
New South		S			X	S	M, S, P, T	
Gotham	E	E, I	E	E	E, I	X	E, I, M, T	E
Capital	M	M	M		M	M	X	M
Mountains					A, E, P		M	X

Legend: A = food, raw & processed, lumber; E = entertainment, tourism, travel; I = investment capital; M = money; P = people, employees & students; S = supply chain services; T = technology; talent & inventions; X = internal transfers.

Comparison of Ecosystems

In this book, I have reflected on the similarities and differences among the eight ecosystems considered, including the trends that appear to be affecting them. As indicated by Table 10.2, these ecosystems are interdependent and progress has often depended on them advancing together rather than in competition. Thus, they should not be viewed as independent samples in the sense one might argue were this a research study, rather than just a report from the field.

I have called each of these ecosystems home for at least one year, and for most of these ecosystems much longer. How are they similar and different? Tables 10.3 and 10.4, repeated from Chapter 1, answer this question in

Table 10.3 Example Innovations

Ecosystem	Example Innovations
Island	Ship design, underwater technologies & weapons
Shining City	Cybernetics, information theory, pragmatism
Heartland	Precision agriculture, vehicle & equipment manufacturing
Old Country	Global trade, water management
New South	AIDS treatment, supply chain management, retail
Gotham	Aviation, communications, computing, energy, fashion, finance
Capital	New Deal, Social Security, Medicare, Medicaid, vaccines
Mountains	Innovation Hubs, forest management, folk art

Table 10.4 Driving Forces and Success Factors

Ecosystem	Driving Forces	Success Factors
Island	Water & blue economy	Good work & delivering results
Shining City	Academic status & awards	Academic outcomes & recognition
Heartland	Agriculture & manufacturing	Good citizenship & outcomes
Old Country	Society & environment	Good citizenship & contributions
New South	Business results & consumption	Business formation & results
Gotham	Money, wealth & consumption	Connections, bluster & stories
Capital	Power & control	Relationships, credibility & deals
Mountains	Community, nature & art	Connecting & mentoring

terms of example innovations of each ecosystem driving forces and success factors affecting innovations.

The example innovations, driving forces, and success factors in these two tables were explained in depth in Chapters 2–9. At this point, it is useful to highlight several contrasts. The examples in Table 10.3 are all rather different. The example innovations for each of the ecosystems have minimal overlaps, with the exception that they all involve people and money. Each ecosystem brings its own value propositions to their marketplaces. Thus, the stories elaborated in Chapters 2–9 are rather different, although there are some structural similarities as outlined at the end of this chapter.

Note that four of the ecosystems are large East Coast cities: Shining City (Boston), New South (Atlanta), Gotham (New York), and Capital (Washington). Over 1,000 miles separate these cities. To a great extent, culture trumps geography in comparing the driving forces and success factors in Table 10.4 for these cities. Consider how these forces and factors differ.

All four cities are driven by pursuits of success. They all seek achievement, but this has different meanings in these four cities, at least as I have experienced these ecosystems. Boston defines itself in terms of academic achievement and accolades, perhaps not a surprise in a state with almost 150 colleges and universities. The higher education sector is the fourth largest in the state's economic base. My sense is that Bostonians see achievement as a means to economic returns, but do not see such returns as the dominant objective.

New York's achievement aspirations are totally focused on money. They are not concerned with producing anything tangible. The goal is money for money's sake. Their success is reflected in their conspicuous consumption. Elegant homes, expensive furnishings, designer clothes, exquisite jewelry, and top of the line cars embody this great emphasis on consumption. New Yorkers like to brag about money, much more so than about advanced degrees. They want to win the wealth game.

Atlanta is also completely focused on money as it accrues from profits creating tangible products, including software for marketing, sales, and operations. Atlantans are proud of the things they create. Their ideas focus more on value creation than just making money. Consumption is also central, particularly in terms of enormous McMansions and high-end vehicles. Wheeling and dealing at boisterous college sporting events is the norm. Business networks are often aligned with alumni and religious affiliations.

Washington is concerned with achievement in terms of power and control. Relationships, personal credibility, and political dealmaking are central. Successful government service can pave paths to much better paying private sector jobs, perhaps later leading to higher-level government positions. Conflicts, infighting, and stalemates are common, but they seem to muddle through, and occasionally do the right things, for example, Social Security and Medicare.

The other four ecosystems include The Island, Heartland, Old Country, and Mountains. These four contexts seem less focused on personal achievement than on society, community, and sustainability. Local concerns tend to be prioritized over personal wealth, perhaps because the opportunities for accruing enormous wealth are limited. We also need to keep in mind the inclinations of the people who choose to live in each of the eight ecosystems. Those inclined to become billionaires would likely immigrate to one of the other four ecosystems, or perhaps to the West Coast.

Values Summary

The rich discussions throughout this book suggest the following, inevitably somewhat simplistic, conclusions regarding the predominant values in each ecosystem:

- The Island – family, work, accomplishment
- Shining City – competing, achieving, accolades
- Heartland – religion, family, country
- Old Country – equity, sustainability, competing
- New South – appearance, conformity, winning
- Gotham – greed, exploitation, wealth
- Capital – power, control, patronage
- Mountains – nature, hospitality, arts

At a personal level, these observations might influence where one wants to live. On a professional level, these observations can inform one's understanding of behavioral and social phenomena likely to be encountered. Successful transitions from one ecosystem to another can require a bit of time to understand the values that predominate.

Innovation Assessments

The eight innovation assessments are contrasted in Figures 10.2–10.5. In Chapters 2–9, I assessed 28 growth opportunities across the eight ecosystems. The four bar graphs in this section provide a compilation of assessments across these growth opportunities.

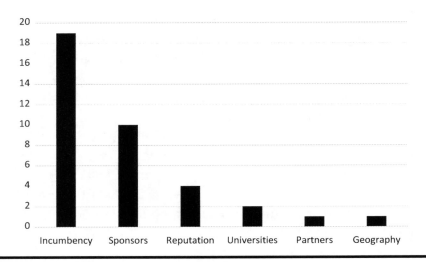

Figure 10.2 Sources of competitive strengths.

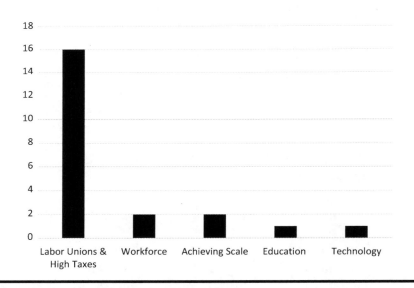

Figure 10.3 Sources of competitiveness weaknesses.

Sources of Competitive Strength

Figure 10.2 indicates that incumbency, existing sponsors, and reputation are the most commonly assessed strengths. University relationships and other partners can be strengths. Geography can sometimes be a strength. Bottom line: it is difficult to have a strong position in a line of business without being in that business.

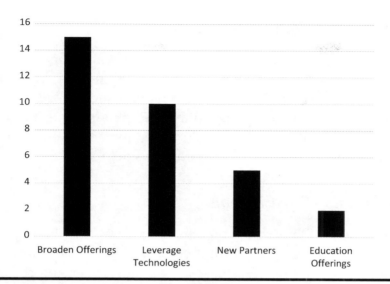

Figure 10.4   Opportunities for competitive advantages.

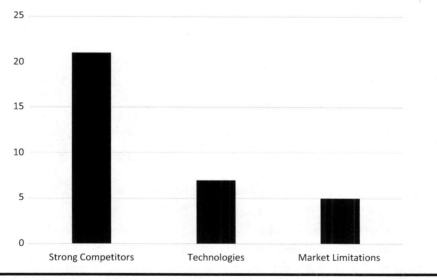

Figure 10.5   Sources of competitive threats.

Sources of Competitiveness Weaknesses

Labor unions and high taxes are the most common sources of weakness as shown in Figure 10.3. This situation is common in major cities in the Northeast and West. Significant strengths are needed to overcome these challenges. Workforce and education deficiencies can also contribute to weakness. Expensive, poorly performing solutions inevitably fail.

Opportunities for Competitive Advantage

Broadening offerings, leveraging technologies, and aligning with new partners can create advantages, as indicated in Figure 10.4. Careful, evidence-based assessments should proceed with such investments. One should carefully monitor such opportunities. Exploiting existing strengths often can proceed on the basis of intuition. Taking advantage of new opportunities requires much more careful consideration.

Sources of Competitive Threats

Figure 10.5 indicates that strong competitors are obvious threats, particularly if they have enabling technologies not yet available to one's firm. Considerations that limit market entry, for example, licensing regulations, can also be threats to the pursuit of opportunities. The nature of threats can influence, for instance, the market segments chosen for the pursuit of new opportunities.

Ecosystem Attributes

How can ecosystems be characterized in general? There is a resource base of geography, knowledge, technology, and money that interacts with educational, government, and private sector enablers, all of which interact with nascent ecosystem innovations.

Figure 10.6, repeated from Chapter 1, provides a summary view of ecosystem attributes as manifested in each of the eight ecosystems. I hasten to note that the brief bulleted lists below each ecosystem name are meant to be representative, not exhaustive. The chapter on each ecosystem provides much more information than can be incorporated into a single figure.

Each of the ecosystems draws upon and influences geography and water, education and knowledge, technology and offerings, money and capital, and culture and politics. As discussed earlier, they all have the Atlantic Ocean in common, even those west of the Eastern Continental Divide – Heartland and western portions of Mountains and New South.

Education and knowledge as well as technology and market offerings differ substantially across ecosystems. For example, agricultural economics is more central to Heartland education and business practices compared to financial economics that is integral to Gotham education and business practices.

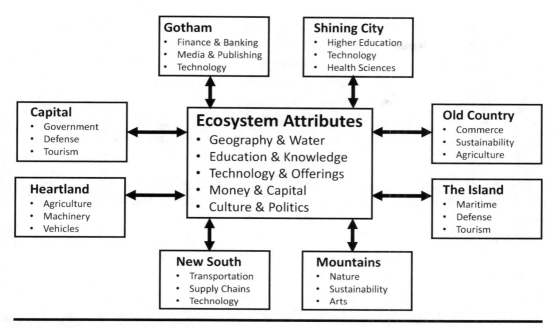

Figure 10.6   Ecosystem attributes.

Culture and politics also vary significantly across ecosystems, as elaborated in discussions in earlier chapters. Red versus blue political differences are of note, but there are also differences that reflect urban versus rural concerns. For example, environmental challenges can be seen quite differently by populations quite close to nature – for example, The Island and Mountains.

Money and capital differ less across ecosystems, due to common currencies and capital markets. Venture capital investments tend to be greater in larger cities such as Gotham and Shining City. In the smaller ecosystems, large infusions of capital are not needed by inherently smaller scale endeavors.

Conclusions

Invention is the creation of a process or device. Innovation is the creation of value in the marketplace, which may include consumers, business to business relationships, or broader constituencies. Innovations may or may not involve inventions. Measures of innovation vary with domains, for example, technology, medicine, and arts. Thus, while the above definition of innovation holds in general, value is manifested in different ways across domains.

The eight ecosystems characterized in Figure 10.6 illustrate the diversity of value propositions, ranging from underwater weapon systems on The Island to precision agriculture in Heartland to folk art and craft beers in Mountains. Such diversity is important across innovation ecosystems. If everyone tried to compete in the same way, everyone would be playing the same game. There would likely be a few big winners and many big losers.

Fortunately, geography, natural resources, climate, and weather combine to discourage copycat innovators. The nature and availability of workforces have significant impacts. The long leadership position in skilled machinist workforces enabled New England to dominate throughout the Second Industrial Revolution. Standardization of equipment, including automation, enabled production with lower skilled workforces, motivating companies to move operations to lower wage southern states.

Similarly, Gotham pioneered many industries that migrated south and west. Thus, market positions can be difficult to defend. Continual investments are needed to improve capabilities and quality, while also reducing costs and prices. Precision agriculture and supply chain optimization are good examples. Innovations need to be continually at the top of enterprise agendas.

Kodak and Polaroid invented but delayed deploying digital photography, not wanting to cannibalize film sales. Digital and Xerox could not believe that people would want personal computers. Motorola and Nokia took turns leading the cell phone market and did not imagine the possibility of iPhones.

Creative destruction, a phrase coined by Austrian economist Joseph Schumpeter, was the result. All six of these high-flying companies withered. Apple, Google, and Microsoft now dominate. In general, we are all better off from such creative destruction. The shareholders of these six companies likely disagreed, but that is how innovation works.

This suggests that the nature of specific innovations is context dependent. However, the process of innovation is rather general, with similar elements across contexts. As I have argued and illustrated in earlier books, the principles and methods of human-centered design are broadly applicable to any context.

Succinctly, human-centered design is a process of considering and balancing the values, concerns, and perceptions of key stakeholders in any endeavor. Stakeholders, attributes, and preferences are central constructs. There are well-honed methods and tools for considering and balancing these constructs.

Nevertheless, context really matters. Having lived in each of the eight ecosystems, a boots-on-the-ground appreciation of an ecosystem is central to understanding the context-specific meaning of the principles and methods of human-centered design. What matters to whom – and why – provides essential insights into how best to foster innovation.

Epilogue

Coming full circle, it would seem that The Island and Mountains have little in common. The Island is dominated by the ocean, while Mountains are commanded by the heights. Yet, there is an interesting connection.

The Breakers is a mansion located on Ochre Point Avenue in Newport. It was built between 1893 and 1895 as a summer residence for Cornelius Vanderbilt II, a grandson of Commodore Vanderbilt, of "robber baron" fame.

The 70-room mansion, with a gross area of 138,300 square feet and 62,482 square feet of living area on five floors, was designed by Richard Morris Hunt in the Renaissance Revival style.

Not to be outdone by his older brother, George Vanderbilt acquired 125,000 acres (200 square miles) in the North Carolina mountains near Asheville. Construction on Biltmore House began in 1889. It was first opened to friends and family on Christmas Eve, 1895.

Biltmore House was designed by architect Richard Morris Hunt and includes 175,000 square feet – more than four acres of floor space. The 250-room French Renaissance chateau includes 35 bedrooms, 43 bathrooms, and 65 fireplaces.

These two magnificent mansions represent the ostentatious proclivities of the Gilded Age, enabled by third-generation Vanderbilt wealth. My guide during my one visit to the Breakers commented, "The first generation makes the money, the second generation manages the money, and the third generation blows it." *Forbes* chronicled this story in 2014.

Index

Pages in *italics* refer to figures and pages in **bold** refer to tables.

Printed in the United States
by Baker & Taylor Publisher Services